At Strategic Coach, we have what we call a No-Entitlement Attitude, which means we believe that you need to create value first before you receive any reward. Profit Works *helps entrepreneurs design an incentive plan that teaches this attitude to your team. I strongly recommend this helpful guide for entrepreneurs who want their employees to think and act like owners!*

— Dan Sullivan, Co-founder and
President of Strategic Coach®

I loved this book. It's an incredibly simple and practical guide to profit sharing and incentives. It's customizable to your organization with great take-a-ways! A must read for any entrepreneurial organization.

— Gino Wickman, Author of *Traction* and
Entrepreneurial Leap

Profit Works *definitely falls into the "I wish I had this years ago" category of a resource that would have been incredibly valuable to my CEO peer group members. A must read and reference for ANY owner/CEO who wants to drive performance in their company.*

— Larry Hart, Vistage Chair (Retired)

I wish I had this book for the previous companies that I owned. We spent a tremendous amount of time trying to figure out a structure for incentive plans and when we finally got it to work, it changed our business. Nearly all of my EOS® clients ask the question: "Is there a model for a great incentive plan?" and now there is. Great work, and a very simple read. I will be purchasing this for all of my clients.

— Coach Bob Shenefelt, Certified EOS Implementer®

We have a good profit-sharing program in place with measurables reported weekly. It feels like an eternity ago that we made Mistake 5: My Incentive Plan Is Disconnected from day-to-day jobs! We have come a long way since those days of giving out bonuses during the holidays that were disconnected from performance-driven rewards. I highly recommend all entrepreneurs read Profit Works *and follow their simple formula! Sharing profits with my well-deserved work family is fun and the favorite part of my job.*

— Sandy King, President of Symbiont Service

Profit Works *reveals a simple and practical way to implement incentive plans in your company. Too many entrepreneurs get stuck here because they can't connect the incentive payout to a unified and collective increase in productivity. This book and its tools provide everything you need to avoid the pitfalls of becoming one of those business owners. I'm recommending the* Profit Works *method to all of the teams I coach.*

— Jill Young, Author of
The Advantage Series books and courses

The great balancing act of creating a challenging, motivating, safe and exciting work climate and culture is a task all leaders take on as elemental to success. Profit Works *shows the reader how to practically approach one of the tough parts of this balancing act: getting a really good incentive plan in place and implemented. This book shows how to avoid the common and even many of the advanced mistakes in the design and execution of incentive pay. Do yourself a favor and use all the ideas in this book you can.*

—John Schuster, Co-author of
The Power of Open-Book Management

Simple and effective! Step-by-step clarity for employees and entrepreneurs. Please do yourself a favor: don't implement a bonus program or incentive-based pay until you have read this book! Use an earned compensation plan instead!

— Don Sasse, Certified EOS Implementer
at High Country NW

All the critical components surfaced in Profit Works *align with companies of ANY size. Clearly defined individual metrics must align with incentive targets that are supported by clarity and consistent, often repeated, communications. It thus makes it possible for everyone to align the needed behaviors to accomplish all personal, team and company goals and expected results."*

— Denise Foley, Chair, Vistage Florida; Former VP of
Procurement, Payroll and Variable Compensation for
AutoNation Inc., a Fortune 200 Company

In this great read, Tom and Alex provide real-world experience and examples that take the mystery out of productivity, engagement and motivation. Readers will discover that motivation comes from a blend of fair incentive programs and organizational culture—all with an eye toward the firm's profitability. They'll learn what works in the financial incentive arena, and more importantly, what doesn't work. I highly recommend Profit Works *to all growth-oriented entrepreneurs.*

— Dr. Dino Signore, President of The Signore Group

Alex and Tom have boiled down and simplified a complex subject, delivering a logical roadmap you can travel with ease. It also supports the 7 Questions Culture and Engagement Framework. *All 7 questions are supported in a well-designed Incentive Plan following this guidance.*

— Walt Brown, Author of *The Patient Organization* and *Death of The Org Chart*

Profit Works *is very helpful and clear on a topic that is often overwhelming for business leaders because it is complicated, emotional and fraught with impact. Thank you, Alex and Tom, for providing a clear explanation, a simple enough road map to apply to real life, and some tools to help us dive into the complexity in a way that gives useful answers.*

— Lynda Martin, Certified EOS Implementer®

PROFIT
WORKS

Unravel the Complexity of **Incentive Plans** to
Increase Employee Productivity,
Cultivate an Engaged Workforce, and
Maximize Your Company's Potential

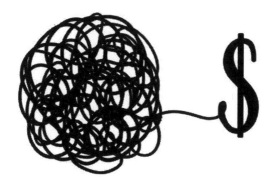

OTHER BOOKS BY THE AUTHORS

What The Heck Is EOS? A Complete Guide for Employees in Companies Running on EOS

Gino Wickman and Tom Bouwer

See the end of this book for a sample chapter.

Achieve Your Vision

Alex Freytag

Look for more books from ProfitWorks in the near future.

PROFIT
WORKS

Unravel the Complexity of Incentive Plans to
Increase Employee Productivity,
Cultivate an Engaged Workforce, and
Maximize Your Company's Potential

ALEX FREYTAG AND TOM BOUWER

AUTHOR ACADEMY elite

Printed in the United States of America

Published by Author Academy Elite
PO Box 43, Powell, OH 43065
www.AuthorAcademyElite.com

LCCN: 2020915480

Paperback ISBN: 978-1-64746-448-6
Hardback ISBN: 978-1-64746-449-3
eBook ISBN: 978-1-64746-450-9

Available in paperback, hardback, e-book, and audiobook

Dedication

To all our clients, coaches and mentors—
past, present and future.
Thank you for trusting us,
for believing in us, and
for serving as a mirror.

TABLE OF CONTENTS

INTRODUCTION

This book is for entrepreneurs and business owners who want to learn how to appropriately incentivize and reward employees for their efforts to make their organization more successful. We use the term "appropriately" because many incentive plans just don't work; they pay out too much (wasted money) or too little (not motivating), they aren't fair, they become expected (i.e., an entitlement), and most of the time, they are too complicated. Regardless of your company's size, this book will give you simple tools and philosophies to design and maximize your incentive plan.

Like so many of you, we recognize that we are standing on the shoulders of giants with this topic. We appreciate those mentors, influencers, and visionaries who shared their time and expertise with us along our journey. We have provided further reading and resources in the back of the book, and we strongly encourage you to tap into these.

This book combines and simplifies the research and our experience. We hope it will inspire you to consider different alternatives and will provide you with specific ideas to create the best incentive plan for *your* organization.

In this book, we use the terms "we" and "you" intentionally: "we" to represent our knowledge and experiences; "you" meaning, well, you. We want you to know we are truly a part of your team as you go down this path. We are passionate about helping entrepreneurs. This is a tricky topic, and at the end of the day, we recognize there's no silver bullet for incentive plans. Know that we are here to help you along the journey.

In this book, we also will use the term "incentive" generically to mean any extra money that is earned by an employee as a result of their changed behavior. This could be profit sharing, an incentive for hitting a certain target, gainsharing, and sales commissions.

Ultimately, recognize that whatever incentive plan you choose to implement, it is one more tool in your toolbox—a powerful tool, but still just one tool. Implemented effectively, the incentive plan is another lever that will help your company increase employee productivity, cultivate an engaged workforce, and maximize your company's potential.

Chapter 1

Why Profit Works

Since 1996, when we first founded ProfitWorks, we have asked employees, "What percent of sales do you think profit is?" Their answers may surprise you; most employees think bottom line profit is 30-50% of sales! While those results would certainly be wonderful, they are not common for most businesses. Upon seeing their employees' answers, one business owner exclaimed, "Are they out of their minds? Do they think I have a money tree in the backyard that I just shake when I want to make more money?"

If your experience is like ours, you know that profit percentages are usually in the single digits, and that profit is incredibly precious. Unfortunately, most employees don't think about this fact as much as you do. They certainly don't see profit numbers as often as you do, if at all. They don't feel connected to profits, and they commonly believe profit is something only the owner or executives need to worry about. Profit is powerful, though, because it funds growth, provides investors and owners with a return, and creates opportunities for employees.

You may have heard profit referred to as the "score at the end of the game." The comparison of business to a game makes it fun and accessible for everyone involved in a company. The game metaphor makes profit that first place trophy that stretches you and your team. The potential for profit can encourage a competitive spirit and the potential for everyone in a company to win (does anyone like to lose?). The fact that profit is typically small, hard to generate, and easy to lose creates what we call positive tension.

Positive tension is that level of anxiety where people are most productive and motivated. The objectives are not so overwhelmingly difficult or unachievable that no one tries. Conversely, they are not so easy that no one cares or puts in any effort. Think about if **Positive tension is that level of anxiety where people are most productive and motivated.** you tried out for an NFL team: making the team is probably not going to happen and as a result, you're not going to be motivated. (Well, you might be motivated to avoid getting hurt.)

Alternatively, think about your state's DMV: there is no motivation because there is no tension, pressure, or anxiety. Each of you will need to find that optimal level of positive tension in your company. Focusing everyone on profit is a great way to do that.

Profit Works for Everyone

Profit works for owners and investors. The potential for profit creates positive tension to generate a return on investment for investors, relative to the risk they have taken. If there is no profit potential, investors typically won't take the risk to invest in the opportunity.

Profit works for your external relationships. It creates tension for you as it pulls against what it costs you to provide your products and services. It stretches you to make smart decisions related to your sourcing relationships as well as to the investments you make to grow your company through innovation, geographic expansion, and new product and/or service development.

Profit works for your employees. When focused on profit, you have the opportunity to create that right level of tension and to increase opportunities for all of your employees (e.g., advancement, learning new skills, increased compensation). When focused on profit, your entire workforce can benefit by understanding this tension. It can create an incredible culture of winning where everyone is focused on generating more profit.

In addition, we've found that companies win when their employees understand how they benefit from being part of a profitable company; they will see the source of new jobs, the opportunities for reinvestment in the business, and their own potential for growth. We've also found that employees are more motivated when they understand the consequences due to a *lack of* profit, from reductions in force (RIFs) to pay cuts to fewer opportunities for professional growth.

Successful companies understand the benefits of creating positive tension or pressure. Tension isn't a bad thing. According to the Yerkes-Dodson Law, performance increases with tension, but only up to a point. When the level of stress becomes too high, performance decreases. So, a moderate amount of tension creates the most buy-in and effort and, therefore, the most productivity. Like a rubber band, you want to stretch your team to grow and reach for something more than mediocrity. Believe it or not, most people want this.

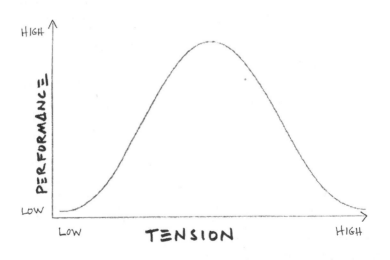

Instilling just enough tension in your culture encourages a higher level of performance. You and your team win when you implement simple and effective tools like weekly meetings full of intense debate and discussion on company issues, and when everyone is accountable. When there's just enough tension in your company, no anchors hold you back from higher performance.

Creating tension in your culture is a blend of art and science. The art is in what tools you decide to teach and how you choose to use those tools. The science comes from using a simple and transparent formula when you design your incentive plan.

Over and over again in client sessions, we hear executives discussing budgeting for bonuses, creating profit-sharing programs, and trying to figure out how to pay employees more so they don't leave for more pay elsewhere. In many cases, though, they're just winging it. There's no clear strategy or methodology for the design. It's often too complicated, not transparent, and has a high degree of subjectivity to it. You may be afraid to draw a line in the sand. You're often shooting from the hip. When incentives aren't truly "earned" and clearly understood, you create an entitlement mentality in your workforce. Entitlement is the death knell for a thriving culture and higher organizational performance.

One of our clients didn't want to follow a formula because she said it might "trap" her. She didn't want to reward under-performing employees. Our question was: "Why are they still with your company?" In the following chapters, we'll give you ideas on how to avoid feeling "trapped."

We encourage you to embrace the intentional philosophies and formulas we share with you in this book. We're capitalists with decades of experience working with hundreds of companies. We've seen what works and what doesn't work. Like you, we want your employees to add more value, to be happy, to be productive and to earn more, and not to get a bigger paycheck for no real reason.

Before we go further, let's provide an example of a simple incentive plan design that works:

- Imagine an annual profit trigger of $1,000,000. Above this amount, the employees can make more by participating in an incentive pool funded by their efforts. Below this, there's no incentive payout.

- Let's say 30% of every dollar above the $1,000,000 trigger goes into the incentive pool. If the company hits $1,500,000 in profits for the year, the incentive pool is $150,000 (30% x $500,000). It can be as simple as that. We'll talk about some ideas for how that gets distributed later.

COMPANY PROFIT (TRIGGER = $1,000,000)	INCENTIVE POOL (30%)	COMPANY PROFIT (AFTER PAYOUT)
$1,000,000	$0	$1,000,000
$1,500,000	$150,000	$1,350,000

KEY TAKEAWAYS

- Most employees think bottom line profit is 30-50% of sales.

- Profit is the score at the end of the game and when everyone is focused on profit, you can create positive tension.

- Profit works for everyone involved in a company including investors, external partners, and employees.

- Successful companies create just the right amount of positive tension in their cultures to create higher levels of performance.

- Successful companies commit to a simple formula when designing an incentive plan.

THINKING QUESTIONS

These are questions to help you slow down and reflect on what you read as well as to help you think about where your head is on the topics discussed in this chapter.

1. What do you think your employees would guess bottom line profit is as a percentage of sales in your company?

    _____

    _____

2. What are three examples of positive tension practices you've implemented in your personal life?

    _____

    _____

    _____

    _____

3. What changes in your own behavior and thinking have you seen as a result?

    _____

    _____

    _____

    _____

Chapter 2

Building a Foundation

Your Mindset

Mitch was one of three owners of a successful, 60-person advertising firm in Texas, and he wanted to put an incentive plan in place. Why? 1) His peers were doing it with great success and 2) it was the latest management trend—everyone was talking about it (even though most didn't really know how to do it).

However, none of the three partners understood nor bought into the fundamental principles necessary for a great incentive plan. They didn't grasp the concept of self-funding. They didn't understand that incentives should change behavior. They didn't have a standard philosophy around raises and instead just gave people what they thought would keep them from leaving the company. They didn't understand the difference between extrinsic and intrinsic motivators. Finally, two of the three partners didn't want to share any financial information with employees.

As you can guess, their plan failed miserably. They paid out a lot of money. Morale and productivity went down. Key people left. All because they didn't go into it with the right mindset.

The foundation of a great incentive plan revolves around five key principles. In Appendix A, there is a short exercise to help you determine your mindset around these principles. An effective incentive plan must:

1) **Be Self-Funded:** An incentive plan must be self-funded. Any additional payout to employees above salary, sales commissions, and COLA (cost of living adjustments) must be the result of their actions above and beyond their normal job responsibilities. Those actions must generate incremental profits that fund the incentive plan. We've yet to find an entrepreneur or business owner who wouldn't pay an extra $150,000 to employees who generated an additional $750,000 in profits due to incremental efforts (again, not just doing their job).

2) **Cause Behavioral Change:** An incentive program must cause a change in behavior. It should create a "we win together" culture. It should motivate employees to look for ways to generate more revenue and profit. It shouldn't be a payout just because they're doing the same old things or getting lucky (more on this in Chapter 3). Once the incentive plan is in place, your employees will come to work with an improved attitude and, as we know, a change in attitude leads to a positive change in behavior. This, however, takes more than an incentive plan; it takes leadership and management. As Gino

Wickman says in *Traction*, "As goes the leadership team, so goes the rest of the organization."

3) **Take into Account Merit-based Raises/COLA:** Significant raises must be merit-based. A person getting a raise must have demonstrated their ability to take on more responsibility and accountability and thus create more value for the company. Every position should have a wage range (outside of sales commissions). For example, if a graphic design artist receives a 1-3% COLA every year, they will soon be *priced* well above the market. When this happens, they are the first people to be let go when times get tough because they're too expensive.

4) **Be both Extrinsic and Intrinsic:** Incentive plans are typically thought of only as extrinsic motivators. It's important to note, though, that when an incentive plan is implemented effectively, it also provides an intrinsic incentive. An example of an intrinsic incentive is, as one of our clients put it, "We have a culture of winning. Just plain winning is as important as any monetary payout." It's intrinsically valuable for people to be part of a winning team. It's about your culture and pride of accomplishment, in addition to improved financial performance. We don't want you to lose sight of the impact of intrinsic motivators when designing and implementing an incentive plan.

5. **Include Information Sharing:** Companies must be willing to share some level of financial information with employees and educate them on what the numbers mean and how each employee impacts them. There

are many ways to do this without sharing every line item from the income statement. We acknowledge this can be scary at first. Another way to think about it, though, is the impact that your employees' lack of knowledge can have on you. If they think you're generating huge profits and that you're keeping it all for yourself, that will lead to actively disengaged and disgruntled employees. We will discuss more on how to share financial information and the importance of education and over-communicating with your employees as a consistent habit in Chapter 6.

If you believe that these five principles are foundational to an effective incentive plan, or even if you're not sure and you'd like to determine where your thinking is, take a few minutes to fill out the Mindset Scorecard in Appendix A, or online at profitworksllc.com. There are no right or wrong answers—it's merely a short thinking exercise.

Incentives motivate and change behavior; bonuses become an entitlement. Our belief, as stated earlier, is that extra pay needs to be earned. We're all about paying employees more, provided they add more value. Our assistant more than doubled her income through an incentive plan, all because she added that much more value. That's really cool! She's more fulfilled, learning more, taking on more responsibility, and her incentive payout reflects her added value.

Let's define that word "value." Merriam-Webster defines value as: "the monetary worth of something." In our context, it means the incremental profit that is the result of someone's actions above and beyond their normal day-to-day job. After all, profit tells us if we are winning or losing the business game.

For example, at the advertising firm mentioned earlier, value could be demonstrated by increasing billing by 5 percentage points. It could also look like a conscientious employee turning off lights and computers, saving thousands in utility bills. It could be creating and implementing a better process that eliminates 30% of touch points and potential dropped balls. It could be increasing sales at an appropriate margin. There are many other examples and we're sure you can think of five things off the top of your head that you'd love to tackle in your business that would drive up profitability. Start with the right mindset, then adopt a standard way of operating your company.

Your Company's Operating System

We've worked with thousands of employees and designed hundreds of incentive plans. In this process, we learned that, assuming you have the right mindset, an incentive plan will never work unless three primary conditions are met:

1. Everyone must be aligned around the same goals: short-term and long-term.

2. Employees must know their numbers and how they can impact their incentive plan.

3. Teams must be open and honest and willing to tackle key issues.

We learned these principles by watching incentive plans fail. Why did they fail? Because at the highest level, these companies didn't have an operating system: a standard way of setting priorities, solving issues, or harnessing their human capital. This discovery took us on a search for an operating system that would help our clients.

We chose EOS®, the Entrepreneurial Operating System® (for an in-depth look at EOS, read *Traction* by Gino Wickman and *What the Heck is EOS?* by Gino Wickman and Tom Bouwer). EOS focuses on three things: Vision, Traction, and Healthy. For this book, we're operating system agnostic; however, you *must have one, and only one* operating system. An operating system will help you define your vision with your leadership team, set long-term and short-term goals, create accountability and discipline throughout your organization, and create a healthy team where everyone is fighting for the greater good.

Everyone in the organization must "buy in" to the vision and the goals. A vision is a plan for where you are going and how you're going to get there. Everyone in the organization must know it. If you asked your employees, "Please tell me our top goals for the year," how many of your employees could truly answer? If they can't, how can you expect them to help drive the business forward? Why would you expect them to care? They need to feel a sense of belonging to something bigger than their day-to-day job. They need a sense of purpose, which is a primary motivator for employees.

> **An operating system will help you define your vision with your leadership team, set long-term and short-term goals, create accountability and discipline throughout your organization.**

In addition, most people want discipline, accountability and a number they know and to which they are held accountable for achieving. Who wants to go home and say to their partner, "Honey, I got paid, but I have no idea what I actually accomplished today"? This employee could be more aware of things like: proposals delivered, number of active clients, days sales outstanding (DSO), utilization, or any other numbers related to their job.

Everyone knowing their number results in several things. First, people know how they impact the organization and their incentive plan. Second, they know if they did a good or bad job. Third, this awareness creates accountability. Fourth, people have a sense of accomplishment. Does everyone in your organization really know their number? Do you have practical tools, consistent training, strong leadership, and exceptional management to help them manage that number? Can they see it on a daily or weekly basis?

A software firm in Georgia implemented this discipline, their employees knew their numbers and bought in, and they saw their profits grow by 60% in one year. Every employee had a scorecard where they tracked at least one number for their job, and, when someone's numbers were off-track, they consistently solved those issues. Employee satisfaction increased and under-performers left. Those are great results, all from each person having and managing their numbers.

Finally, every organization needs to be healthy. This is defined as everyone fighting for the greater good and having vulnerability-based trust, as defined by Patrick Lencioni in his book, *The Five Dysfunctions of a Team*. Vulnerability-based trust must exist in order for management to share information with employees, and it must exist for a team to have healthy conflict about business issues. Healthy conflict can only exist when there is a psychological safety net so team members can debate and solve important issues without it getting personal. This encourages trust, which gets your employees invested in the business and is critical for any incentive plan.

Imagine if 90% of your employees came to work each day very committed to doing their best, moving the organization forward, and generating more value. We know it sounds ideal. To those of you who believe, "My employees don't give a @#%*!," we ask you to keep an open mind because we've seen it work time and time again.

Key Takeaways

- Some degree of belief in the 5 mindset principles of incentive plans is critical:

  1. Incentive plans must be self-funded.

  2. Effective incentive plans can change behavior.

  3. You must have a consistent philosophy on raises related to added value.

  4. Effective incentive plans are a blend of both extrinsic and intrinsic motivators.

  5. Successful companies share some level of financial information with employees.

- You must choose one and only one operating system.

- Everyone needs to be aligned around the same short-term and long-term goals.

- Everyone must know how they impact their incentive plan and how they contribute.

- Teams should be healthy, open, and honest.

THINKING QUESTIONS

1. On a scale of 1 to 10, how comfortable are you sharing financial information with your employees? (1 is very uncomfortable; 10 is very comfortable) _____

2. Write down your top three concerns with sharing financial information with employees.

   a. _____

   b. _____

   c. _____

3. What financial information have you shared in the past, and with whom did you share it?

   _____

   _____

4. If your employees know you make a 9% profit, and they originally might have guessed it to be closer to 50%, how might that be an advantage to you?

   _____

   _____

5. Is your company running on one operating system? If so, which one?

   _____

   _____

Chapter 3

Incentive Plan Mistakes

Business owners and executives typically make a combination of mistakes when developing an incentive plan. This not only leads to frustration on the part of leaders and employees, but also causes them to lose confidence in the effectiveness of incentives in general; these mistakes ultimately result in failed incentive plans. Here are six common mistakes people make when designing an incentive plan:

1. **It's Too Complex:** Simplicity is the #1 key when designing an incentive plan. If the plan is too complex and difficult to explain, your employees will neither understand nor trust the plan. Complicated plans are also time-consuming and difficult to administer.

2. **It's Discretionary:** If the payout is subject to whatever you're feeling at the moment, it's more of an emotional reaction than a strategic one; you're just winging it. Discretionary plans create an entitlement mentality because often, these types of plans pay out even when the company misses targets. Further, employees feel they have no control because there is a weak link between what they do every day and the discretionary payout.

3. **It Creates Silos:** Setting up an incentive plan that pits departments against each other creates divisions in your company. We'd even suggest removing the word "division" from your company vocabulary because words matter. You could call your departments business units, teams, or groups. You are one company with a unified team and one voice. You don't want an incentive plan that drives wedges or builds silos within your company. This is true even if you have multiple locations or groups.

MKTG   SALES   CUST. SERV.   OPERATIONS   FINANCE

4. **It's Unattainable:** If you tie your incentive plan to unattainable goals, your team won't be motivated to really go for it. Many times, although you believe the goals are attainable, your employees may not because they haven't been taught about inefficiencies, waste and growth opportunities. They don't know about all the potential that is in your business. More on this in Chapter 7.

5. **It's Disconnected from Their Day-To-Day Jobs:** If your employees don't know what drives the plan and don't understand how profit works at your company, then there's no link between the work they're doing every day and its impact on your incentive plan. You must help them understand the basics of profit and cash to tie their daily activities to the potential payout.

6. **It Has No Perceived Value:** If the potential payout is too small, it won't be motivating; too large, and it's a waste of money. It can also be the wrong type of incentive—some people want cash, and some people want tickets to a football game or an extra day off.

The following stories are all real-life examples. They may provide some additional insight.

MISTAKE 1: MY INCENTIVE PLAN IS TOO COMPLEX

 The owner of a precision plastics manufacturer wanted to incentivize his employees to drive more profitability. Two historical pain points in his business were scrap and rework, so he designed the plan around improving those two numbers, along with on time delivery.

He wanted to include all employees in a payout, so he tied the front office employees to a discretionary plan, with the controller's bonus tied to accounts receivable. "It was such a twisted, complicated mess," he recalled. "I spent a frustrating amount of time just administering the plan and trying to keep it fair." After the second year, he discontinued the plan when the company lost money, but he still had to pay out bonuses to a few departments because they had actually hit their departmental numbers.

> We'd even suggest removing the word "division" from your company vocabulary because words matter.

The owner threw his hands up at the whole situation. "I thought, 'I can't win!' and I almost changed the rules on the incentive plan after seeing the company's profits falling mid-year," said the owner. The departments were hitting their various metrics and getting these generous payouts, but the company was basically breaking even. He knew, though, that changing the rules would kill the team's trust in him, so he decided to take his expensive lumps this time, with the hope of preserving his credibility long-term.

Eventually, he realized the plan was too complex and the employees didn't really know how they impacted the plan.

Mistake 2: My Incentive Plan is Discretionary

 When another business owner set up his first bonus plan, he knew it wasn't the best plan. Still, he wanted to share some of the profits from his Ohio-based metal solution manufacturing company with his employees each year. He set it up so that he had to decide who would get how much based on how *he felt* they contributed during the year. He knew it was discretionary, but as he shared, he "wanted the employees to be rewarded when the company did well." In reality, this was a bonus plan, not an incentive plan.

A similar analogy is the participation trophy. When your daughter gets an award just for showing up or gets a twelfth place trophy, it doesn't help her develop her sense of confidence, self-esteem, or pride of accomplishment. This only happens if there's a chance for failure. To fail is to grow and learn.

After a few years, this same leader felt like the bonus had started to be regarded as a holiday bonus with no real tie to whether the company made or lost money. He also witnessed a "Santa Claus effect" as he saw employees on their best behavior around the holidays because they knew he was trying to figure out bonuses.

The plan didn't change behavior because it was discretionary, and the employees didn't know how their actions impacted the results. The employees had come to expect the bonus because they'd always gotten it. In 2017, when there were no profits to share, the leader decided not to pay anything out. "They were pissed," he said. "They thought because they'd always gotten the bonus before, they'd always get it." Like Clark Griswold in the movie *Christmas Vacation*, one guy had already spent the bonus on a swimming pool because he'd expected to get it. The owner was flabbergasted. The bonus plan had truly become an entitlement.

Mistake 3: My Incentive Plan Creates Silos

MKTG   SALES   CUST. SERV.   OPERATIONS   FINANCE

At a large plumbing supply distributor in the Northeast, each location's general manager was offered incentives based on their respective branch's performance. As a result, there was no cooperation or sharing of best practices. Each branch operated independently. The owner had succeeded in pitting the branches against each other. They were competing for people and other resources instead of working together as a team.

The CEO also realized that the incentives didn't create a common culture or drive cooperation between branches. "I realized that some branches weren't sharing products with others because they thought they could sell it at some point when the other branch had a guaranteed sale," she said. She realized she'd created the quintessential *siloed* organization. An additional consequence was that she had to pay out bonuses to one of the branches when the company lost money that year. "Our new incentive plan quickly changed that," she said.

MISTAKE 4: MY INCENTIVE PLAN IS UNATTAINABLE

An executive, who was *not* in sales, worked for a large, multi-national company where 60% of his compensation was based on an incentive plan. He had no input or buy-in to the incentive plan goals; they were dictated by the corporate office in France. The company set goals that were so out-of-this-world, he knew he could never achieve them. He told us, "I'm taking a 60% pay cut because these goals are ridiculous. I've got kids in school, a house, and a car. I'm going to find another job." Two months later, he had another job. He left the company because his incentive was unattainable.

MISTAKE 5: MY INCENTIVE PLAN IS DISCONNECTED FROM DAY-TO-DAY JOBS

The owner of a GeoThermal Pool Heating and AC company in Florida felt she had a great bonus plan. She'd had it for several years, and it paid out consistently each year around the holidays. She didn't communicate with her workforce, though. Everyone was fulfilling their roles and seemed focused. They enjoyed the payouts, but as she thought more about what kind of culture she wanted to create at her company, she realized the team was playing a game without a way to keep score. They had no idea if they were winning or losing.

She felt that the culture lacked energy and a drive for excellence or improvement. People seemed like zombies just going through the motions. She realized her team was disconnected. Because she wasn't communicating anything about the plan or her company's performance, her employees didn't know what measurables (or numbers, KPIs, metrics—we'll use measurables to mean all of these things for consistency) drove the plan, and they didn't understand how profit *works* at her company. There was no link between the work they were doing every day and the payouts they were receiving at the end of each year.

Mistake 6: My Incentive Plan has No Perceived Value

The owner of a landscape company felt she had a great bonus plan. She'd had it for several years, and it consistently paid a conservative amount to the employees each year around the holidays. She eventually realized the problem when she surveyed the employees about the plan— it wasn't enough money to motivate them. It was only a bonus, a gift. One employee recalled, "A few hundred bucks at the end of the year is nice and all . . . but knowing it was coming didn't cause me to do anything differently throughout the year." It's critical to design a plan that pays employees enough to get their attention and to interest them in changing their behavior.

Between incentives that are either minuscule, with no perceived value, or incentives tied to unattainable goals, how do you design and communicate a plan that will truly motivate everyone? How do you stretch the team, protect the company in the event of a downturn, keep it simple and fair, have some fun, *and* pay out enough to drive changed behavior? It's like trying to solve a Rubik's Cube or spin seventeen plates at the same time!

The primary purpose of an incentive plan is to positively direct employee behavior toward improving the company's financial performance. We all recognize that setting rewards for achieving a goal will influence behavior. It's simply that most of us don't know how to design a simple *and* effective plan. As owners and executives, most of us are making it up as we go, or reinventing the wheel, all while hoping the incentive plan we design will manage our people. The truth is, the plan won't manage your people—*you* need to do that. We can't abdicate the hard work it takes to communicate the plan—whatever the design—and to reinforce it consistently. Most importantly, we must provide our workforce with all the necessary tools and training it takes for them to become active participants in finding the money to fund the plan.

The truth is, the plan won't manage your people—you need to do that.

If we take the time to design a **simple** plan and invest the time to teach our employees how they can put more money in their pockets by pulling certain levers, driving certain measurables on their scorecards, completing their quarterly priorities (sometimes called Rocks), and being disciplined about their weekly meetings and issue processing, we can create a plan that generates *earned compensation,* **not** an entitlement plan.

Key Takeaways

- When designing an incentive plan, business owners typically make a combination of mistakes including: making it too complex, making it discretionary, creating silos, making the goals unattainable, keeping it disconnected from day-to-day activities, and making the payouts too small.

- The primary purpose of an incentive plan is to positively shape employee behavior toward improving the company's financial performance.

- An incentive plan won't manage your people; you need to do that.

- It takes time and intention to teach your employees how they impact the incentive plan and to provide tools for them to actively contribute to the plan.

- An effective incentive plan generates *earned* compensation for your employees.

Thinking Questions

1. Think about a past incentive plan you've been involved with. How effective was it and did it motivate you?

    _____

    _____

    _____

    _____

2. If you currently have an incentive plan, is it helping to positively shape the behavior of your employees? If so, what are two examples you have seen?

    _____

    _____

    _____

    _____

3. Have you ever paid out an incentive or bonus even though the goal wasn't hit? How did that make you feel?

    _____

    _____

    _____

    _____

CHAPTER 4

DESIGN OPTIONS

In this chapter, we'll share three simple incentive plan design options for you to consider:

1. A Profit-Based Design

2. A Profit Pail Design

3. A Top Line Trigger Design

Each option has advantages and disadvantages and will be individually appropriate for different companies and different situations. Keeping it simple is the key to designing a good incentive plan. When the design is simple, it's easier to explain and administer, and this clarity and simplicity helps your workforce trust the plan.

The algorithm for creating an effective incentive plan has three simple steps. Follow these steps before the plan is launched and communicated to the company:

1. Establish a TRIGGER.

2. Determine the SHARE above the trigger.

3. Decide WHO is included in the plan.

We're often asked, "When is the best time to design and roll out an incentive plan?" Although there's no perfect time, most business owners with whom we have worked target the rollout toward the end of the calendar year for the upcoming year. However, there's nothing wrong with introducing an incentive plan mid-year.

Step 1: Establish a TRIGGER.

A trigger is a minimum threshold that must be achieved before a payout pool is generated. The trigger must be high enough to protect the company, but not so high as to be perceived as unattainable. The big benefit of designing a plan with this simple gatekeeping formula is that it focuses everyone on one number. That number is the score at the end of the game. In this way, establishing an incentive plan is essentially making business a fun and exciting game.

Why do people play games? People play games to win. People play games to have fun. And it's certainly a lot more fun when we're winning. To know if we're winning or not, we have to keep score. In business, we keep score with the financial statements, which tell us numbers like profit, cash, or equity. These lagging indicators are important to the game of business, but without a connection to these numbers, it's still hard for an employee to know how their role impacts them.

Often, your employees are too disconnected from these financial statements. As you move forward, identify activity-based numbers in your company to serve as leading indicators for everyone's work. Then, teach your employees how those leading indicators impact the lagging outcomes found on the financial statements, including the trigger. We'll provide some ideas on how to do this in Chapter 6.

Why do people play games? People play games to win. People play games to have fun. And it's certainly a lot more fun when we're winning.

Step 2: Determine the SHARE above the trigger.

Once the company has hit the trigger, the payout formula kicks in. The basic formula is simply establishing a percent or dollar amount over that trigger that goes into the incentive pool. The science behind deciding this involves a few questions you'll need to answer, along with some of our research. We'll talk about this in the sections below.

Step 3: Decide WHO is included in the plan.

We strongly encourage you to design a plan that includes all employees. When you run on an operating system, you have a clear vision, and you're consistently working on getting that vision shared by everyone: not just shared with everyone but shared by everyone. Everyone means all people, from the leadership team to the frontline. You want to create a unified team, like rowers in a crew shell, all grabbing an oar, and all contributing to the progress and success of the team—winning together, failing together here and there, but inevitably growing together.

PROFIT-BASED DESIGN

The most common form of incentive plan design is based on reaching a profit trigger. The profit trigger you establish needs to allow your company to meet its basic obligations: return on investment (ROI) for the risk-takers (investors/owners), taxes, capital investment, and debt obligations. We love this design because profit truly is the score at the end of the game. A profit-based plan works for everyone.

Once the company has hit the trigger, the payout formula kicks in. The basic formula is to establish a percentage of incremental profits over that trigger that goes into the incentive pool. For example, if your trigger is $2,000,000 and your percentage share above the trigger is 30%, then 30% of every dollar above the $2,000,000 goes into the incentive pool.

The goal is to create a pool that's large enough to be meaningful to the employees when paid out, but not so large that you're rewarding excessively with little relationship to changed behavior. With the law of diminishing returns, there's a point at which an increase in payout won't result in the commensurate increase in productivity. This is perhaps more art than science, but our experience is that an incentive pool between 5% and 15% of wages starts to get interesting for employees, but only if the company is surpassing its profit trigger.

For example, if someone making $60K per year has an opportunity to *earn* an additional $6K, this becomes very interesting. "What do I need to do to get that?" asked one employee. That's the curiosity we're looking for.

In most cases, your company will share anywhere between 5% and 50% of the incremental profits above the trigger, with the company keeping the rest of the incremental profit. Once you know your total annual payroll dollars, it's easy math to figure out what this ballpark target number will be.

With a simple spreadsheet, you can play around with the trigger and the percentage share. Run through some scenarios and variations as you consider the company obligations mentioned above, the economy, the team's current engagement, and how much time you plan to spend providing and reinforcing the tools and training. In our experience, it may take you 30 minutes to draft this initial plan.

As an example, one year, the owner of a precision plastics manufacturer had a stretch target of $600,000 in annual profits on $3 million in sales. He wanted to design a profit-sharing plan that included all employees. He decided to set his trigger at a realistic $300,000 and to share 10% of everything above that, with no cap. If the company were to hit the $600,000 stretch budget, each employee would get about 10% of their annual wages.

Here are a few notes, caveats, exceptions, etc.:

- When you communicate the plan, be sure to let everyone know that this is the plan for this year only. Next year, the goals will most likely be different. The trigger may be higher or lower. The percentage share above the trigger may be higher or lower as well. It should be communicated that each year, the trigger and/or the percentage above the trigger may be different, based on what's going on at the company and in the economy.

- Many companies are seasonal, and they may decide that the trigger is different for each quarter. This is fine, as long as you communicate this in a simple message to everyone when you roll out the plan. However, if you have a seasonal business, it may make sense to consider the Profit Pail design described below instead.

- We generally don't suggest capping the payout, which isn't to say you shouldn't, but it would be the exception, not the rule. For example, if you have an employee stock ownership plan (ESOP), it may make sense. In this case, the ESOP is serving as the long-term incentive for all the employee-owners at the company, while the profit-based incentive plan is creating a short-term line of sight for your team. For more information on ESOPs, visit www.nceo.org.

- Profit is meaningless if a business runs out of cash. If cash flow is or has ever been a consistent issue, consider an accounts receivable (AR) target or a cash amount target as an additional gatekeeper to the incentive payout. Sometimes this kind of gatekeeper may be required by shareholders, boards, or bank covenants. For example, if your trigger is $1.5 million, you might decide that the incentive plan payout is not activated unless AR is below 5% of revenue. It doesn't make sense for your firm to borrow money to pay an incentive. If your company is truly healthy and profitable, then cash should be available. You can also select the timing of the payout based on when you typically have more cash.

- Your company can have a year with extraordinary results due to some unforeseen event. Therefore, it makes sense to communicate to the workforce something to the effect that: "Management reserves the right to exclude extraordinary events from the payout formula." Be cautious about this one, as you don't want to damage trust by being perceived as having changed the rules in the middle of the game. However, most employees will find this reasonable and understandable. We discuss this further in Appendix C: Incentive Plans in Scary Times.

- Companies with multiple locations can reward locations separately, provided the overall company meets its objectives and numbers. Again, communication is the key. A company doesn't want to pay out huge incentives to one location when, overall, the company isn't meeting its objectives. A variation is to reward the location with a percentage of the incentive (e.g., 50%) if they hit their goals and the remaining percentage if the overall company hits theirs. This does make it more complicated and doesn't really promote a team approach, so be cautious here.

- Some companies want to reward leaders and managers above and beyond the rest of the workforce. You can design a second leadership and management incentive plan using the same format and include the leadership and management team in both incentive pools. Just be sure to let everyone know that there's a separate leadership pool because, well, they're going to find out anyway. Hopefully, this motivates them to strive for bigger and better roles in your company. Payout methods are described in more detail in Chapter 5.

PROFIT PAIL DESIGN

If your business does not have consistent month-to-month profitability, but you can frequently track and predict sales, gross margin, and profit, consider the Profit Pail Design. Steve Wilson has done a lot of work in this area with his "Bucket Bonus Plan."

In this type of design, the incentive pool is *not* tied to the calendar, but rather, it's tied to a percentage (or dollar amount) of profit in a predefined "pail." For example, when the Profit Pail hits $100,000, 10% or $10,000 goes to the employees. This can happen once a year or 10 times a year—it just depends on how much profit is generated. As you can see, rather than the calendar being the trigger, the trigger is a full pail of profit, and this starts with the first dollar of profit.

To design this plan, the first step is to determine the dollar amount of pretax profit you want for the year. Since the plan must be self-funded, you'll need to surpass your planned profit and pay the incentive out of *incremental profits* over the plan threshold. Divide your *stretch* profit dollars for the year by the number of times you'd like to pay out per year.

A common range of payouts is between 6 and 10. The frequency of the payouts affects not only your employees' level of engagement, but also your communication pulse to your team, so this is an important consideration. Adjust this profit number to a round number for simplicity, and this becomes the size of the pail.

To determine the incentive pool, decide the share (i.e., how much of each pail gets paid out). We suggest using an increasing percentage of each pail throughout the year to keep future, larger pails motivating and in sight. By doing this, you're also protecting the company in the event of a downturn later in the year.

For example, you might allocate 5% of the first pail to the incentive pool, 10% of the second pail, and so forth. Verify the pail dollar amounts, testing the plan in a spreadsheet before rolling it out. Ensure that the dollars pulled from all pails total a percentage of total wages that's meaningful (again, the ideal range is 5% to 15% of total wages).

Let's look at an example: the owner of a seasonal Wisconsin landscaping company with 75 employees and a payroll of $3.5 million wanted to set up a Profit Pail plan. In the prior year, her firm made $900K in profit, but she knew it should be closer to $2.8 million.

To establish a consistent pail size, we used her *stretch* profit target of $2.8 million. She decided to set up seven pails of $400K each. The first pail funded the incentive pool at 5% of the pail, the second and third pails were at 10%, the fourth was at 15%, and the fifth and sixth were at 20%, with the seventh maxing out at 25% of the profits in that last pail.

It's clear from this Profit Pail example that a spreadsheet will be incredibly useful and save you time, allowing you to test assumptions and different scenarios. Another advantage of this design is that you can imagine the potential for visual tracking scoreboards and other fun, colorful, publicly displayed progress charts.

Reflecting on this method, keep in mind that this begins to get more complicated to explain. The more complicated it is to explain, the less your team will understand it, and the less likely they will be to trust it. Based on our experience, you'll likely want to explain this plan many times, with rollout information and other supporting documentation, always over-communicating. Then, people will have every opportunity to ask questions, understand how the plan is designed, and more importantly, understand how to maximize it.

Top Line Trigger Design

In businesses that are consistently profitable and where most employees don't control pricing or have a big impact on expenses, it can make sense to design a simple incentive plan focused on top line revenue.

For example, in many highly profitable professional service businesses, such as wealth management, consulting, staffing, and other service firms, where most of the revenue generation is happening due to the efforts of one person or a small group of people, it can be impactful to design a simple incentive plan based on hitting a top line trigger.

We have this type of plan for our company, and it's effective. Our assistant really doesn't impact costs (much) or pricing (at all). Day in and day out, she supports us in driving revenue by keeping our clients happy and helping us get new clients. In this type of situation, a top line trigger incentive plan makes sense. It also keeps us from dealing with the complexity of designing bonuses for our assistant based on activity-based measurables, which, as we mentioned above, can result in paying out incentive payments to employees when the overall company hasn't hit its goals.

Similar to the profit-based design, the priority is keeping it simple. In this case, the trigger is a top-line revenue target that's realistic and helps the owners achieve their goals while also protecting the company in the event of a downturn. Many times, this is simply the budgeted revenue target for the year.

Determine your total payroll for all those involved in the incentive plan so you can use this as a guide for the incentive pool. Again, use 5-15% of wages as a ballpark target payout amount if the company is hitting its stretch goal.

Once the company has hit the revenue trigger, the payout formula kicks in. With this design, we suggest using a fixed dollar amount for the payout amount once the target has been surpassed. This keeps it simple, you can budget for it, and everyone is on the same page.

Here are a few notes, caveats, exceptions, etc.:

- With this type of design, because you aren't basing it on the company's profit, which is the score at the end of the game, consider adding a profitability target as a gatekeeper that has to be met for the payout to be triggered.

- Similarly, if cash flow is or has ever been a consistent issue at your company, consider an accounts receivable (AR) target or a cash dollar amount target as a gatekeeper to paying out the incentive. It doesn't make sense for your firm to borrow money to pay an incentive. If the company is truly healthy and profitable, then cash should be available.

- Be sure to talk with your accountant to cover the tax implications of your incentive plan design.

KEY TAKEAWAYS

- Three simple incentive plan design options to consider are a Profit-Based Design, a Profit Pail Design, and a Top Line Trigger Design.

- There are three simple steps to create an effective incentive plan: establish a trigger, determine the share above the trigger, and decide who is included in the plan.

- A trigger is a minimum threshold that must be achieved before a payout pool is generated.

- The share is the percent or dollar amount over the trigger that goes into the incentive pool.

- Effective incentive plans include all employees in the plan.

- In a Profit-Based Design, establish a profit trigger that allows your company to meet its basic obligations for return on investment, taxes, capital investment, and debt obligations.

- In a Profit Pail Design, the incentive pool is not tied to the calendar, but rather to a percentage or dollar amount of profit in a predefined "pail."

- In a Top Line Trigger Design, a fixed dollar amount is the payout pool once a certain revenue target is achieved.

Thinking Questions

1. Which of these incentive plan design options resonates with you the most and why?

   _____

   _____

   _____

2. What are your next 3 steps to put an incentive plan in place in your company?

   _____

   _____

   _____

3. As you think about the leaders and managers in your company today, what are your biggest concerns?

   _____

   _____

   _____

4. How effective are your teams?

   _____

   _____

   _____

Chapter 5

Payout Options

Regardless of which incentive design you decide to use, after the trigger is hit, there will be an incentive pool that needs to be divvied up. Of course, if your company doesn't pass the trigger in a quarter or a year, there are no payouts. Not paying out can be an emotional decision, but it's paramount to staying disciplined and avoiding an entitlement mentality among employees.

With the theme of simplicity in mind, your payout method must be an algorithm. Using a simple formula helps take emotion and subjectivity out of the payout event and strengthens trust. Two important considerations are payout timing and payout method.

Payout Timing

Note: This section applies only to the Profit-Based Design and the Top Line Trigger Design; as we stated, the payout timing in the Profit Pail Design is determined by filling a pail.

As you consider your payout timing, think for a moment about your workforce. Elliott Jaques, a Canadian psychoanalyst, social scientist, and management consultant, teaches that different people have different timespan capacities.

Imagine a timespan continuum. On one end are people who can visualize a distant future, seeing 10 years or more ahead; visionary entrepreneurs like Steve Jobs and Jeff Bezos are good examples. On the other end of that continuum are people who don't or can't look out much further than tomorrow or next week. They may live paycheck to paycheck and aren't saving a lot for their future. Where on the continuum does your workforce live?

TIMESPAN CONTINUUM

| 1 DAY | THE NEXT PAYCHECK | 90 DAYS | 1 YEAR | 5 YEARS | 10+ YEARS |

With this in mind, we suggest you structure your payout method with the timespan capacity of your workforce in mind. Monthly payouts require more administration and payouts may be smaller and less impactful, so we suggest quarterly payouts. This frequency also aligns perfectly with the 90-Day World® created for companies that are running on EOS or other operating systems. Assuming you've surpassed the trigger for the quarter, calculate that quarter's pool based on the formula you decided on within the design you chose.

Recall the example from the small plastics manufacturer: the owner designed a plan that paid out 10% of incremental profits over an annual trigger of $300K, such that each quarter's trigger was $75K. When the company generated $125K in profits in the first quarter, which was $50K in incremental profits over the trigger, 10% ($5,000) of that went into the pool.

If you structure your plan as a quarterly plan like this one, consider banking 50% of each of the first three quarters' payouts, with a catch-up amount paid after the completion of the year. This creates enough of an incentive to keep everyone's head in the game quarterly and protects the company in the event of a sub-par quarter later in the year.

To protect the company, the plastics company owner held back 50% of the first quarter's payout and clearly communicated the what, how, and why of this at his Q1 State of the Company meeting. He shared the *score* and the reward, with intention, which helped keep the team's head in the game. After the first quarter, each of his ten employees received $250 and understood what they needed to do for the remainder of the year to continue to earn quarterly payouts and to earn that banked amount as well.

Paying out annually works too. If you decide to pay out annually, just be sure to report on what the *score* is during your quarterly State of the Company meetings. These are quarterly meetings where you share company and incentive plan information with your employees. They don't need to be long, just 15-30 minutes. Let your team know what the incentive pool looks like throughout the year. There's nothing worse than playing a game and not knowing the score. We discuss ideas for the format of your quarterly company update meetings in more detail in Chapter 7.

Here are a few notes, caveats, exceptions, etc.:

- To qualify for the payout, an employee must be in good standing with the company. This typically means that they align with the core values, are in the right seat, and they're not on a performance improvement plan or undergoing disciplinary action.

- Employees must be employed on the date of the incentive payout. Be sure to include this in your incentive plan documents.

- Most companies will also put a timeline around qualifying. Usually employees must be employed for 90 days. Some align with other benefit criteria, like a 401(k) plan qualification, to keep it simple.

- When communicating the incentive payout potential to employees, be sure to let them know that this is pretax income.

Payout Methods

There are a few payout methods to consider. Your choice depends on several factors, including the size of your company, what type of culture you're trying to create, what message you're trying to send,

If your company doesn't pass the trigger in a quarter or a year, there are no payouts.

and what feels right. We'll describe in more detail the advantages and disadvantages of each method below. We suggest these choices:

1. Percentage of Wages Payout

2. Equal Payout

3. Hybrid Payout

PERCENTAGE OF WAGES PAYOUT

The percentage of wages payout method is the most common choice of our clients, and as with all payout methods, there are advantages and disadvantages to consider. With this method, you first determine the total payroll of all those involved in the plan, which becomes your denominator. Each employee's wage is the numerator. Whatever percentage an employee's wage is of total wages is the percentage of the incentive pool they'll receive if the company surpasses the trigger. This keeps the payout dollar amount in alignment with the perceived value of each position in your company.

	% OF TOTAL PAYROLL	% OF INCENTIVE POOL	INCENTIVE POOL (EXAMPLE)	EMPLOYEE PAYOUT
EMPLOYEE WAGE	$60,000	2%	$150,000	$3,000
TOTAL PAYROLL	$3,000,000			

Under this method, someone with a $50k salary would get half as much as someone with a $100k salary. On a percentage basis, though, they'd be getting the same percentage of their salary. The thought behind this is that higher-paid employees have more responsibility and (hopefully) more impact on profits.

This method isn't as transparent as the equal payout method described below. Still, you can certainly speak openly about the percentage of wages everyone is getting, and your employees have a relative sense of their expected payout. With this method, it's arguably easier to *hide* in the business and still get a payout. As we've said several times before, though, an incentive plan won't manage your people—you and your managers still have to do that.

EQUAL PAYOUT

With an equal payout method, every employee gets the same dollar amount. The incentive pool is divided by the total number of people qualified for the payout, which is typically all employees. Again, typically the employee must be in good standing and have been with the company for more than 90 days.

If your organization is smaller and flatter, this payout method can be quite impactful. The advantages are that it's easy to administer and communicate and to do so with complete transparency.

Our Florida GeoThermal Pool Heating client used this formula for her team and loved the results. And it wasn't only the cultural impact. She said, "We exceeded the budgeted revenue goal by 17.8% for total revenues. This is our highest revenue since I started in this business in 1984. In addition to higher revenues, our profit % was awesome, enabling a company-wide profit share of $126,000, which we shared quarterly throughout the year. We completed the final payout in February."

We've witnessed this payout method creating a stronger degree of peer-to-peer accountability as well. The transparency encourages all team members to contribute and pull their weight because everyone knows what everyone else is getting. There's a great degree of openness and a unified feeling that they're all on the same team.

As we've said before, you don't want to subsidize poor performance. So, in an equal payout environment, your message to the team must be that "you can't quit and stay," meaning an employee can't collect the incentive without adding value. The plan won't manage your people; your managers will still have to do this. They will have to make the tough people decisions by being great leaders and managers. It goes without saying: it all starts at the top.

HYBRID PAYOUT

A third payout method is a hybrid payout. It's a combination of the two methods listed above and encompasses the benefits of both. A common way to structure a plan using this method is to allocate 40% of the pool to an equal payout method, where everyone gets the same dollar amount. The remaining 60% of the pool is distributed using the percentage of wages method. Of course, these percentages can be tweaked to suit your situation.

The great advantage of this design has to do with the messaging you send with this type of hybrid payout. You've got a little "We Comp" (40%) and a little "Me Comp" (60%). You're able to talk transparently about the dollar amount in the *We* pool, advocating teamwork and a sense of camaraderie, and you'll keep the payout more in alignment with wages.

You can continue to promote the accountability that the Equal Payout method highlights while paying more to those who make more money due to their role. This method is also effective because underperformers are often encouraged to leave the company as a healthy culture expunges them. A caution is that it adds a bit more complexity to describing the plan and takes more time to administer, but we feel the advantages far outweigh those disadvantages.

Key Takeaways

- When considering payout options, two important considerations are payout timing and payout method.

- The payout timing for the Profit Pail Design is determined by how fast the pails are filled.

- The best practices for payout timing are quarterly or annually, depending on the line of sight of your workforce.

- Three payout methods to consider are percentage of wages payout, equal payout, and a hybrid approach.

- With a percentage of wages payout, whatever percent an employee's wage is of total wages is the percentage of the incentive pool they'll receive if the company surpasses the trigger.

- With an equal payout, every employee gets the same dollar amount. It's easy to administer and communicate and drives a strong degree of peer-to-peer accountability.

- A hybrid payout method is a combination of an equal payout method and the percentage of wages method. Often 40% of the pool is allocated to the equal payout method and the remaining 60% is distributed using the percentage of wages method.

- If your company doesn't pass the trigger in a quarter or a year, there are no payouts.

THINKING QUESTIONS

1. Which of these payout options resonates with you the most and why?

   _____

   _____

   _____

2. What obstacles do you foresee with your preferred payout option?

   _____

   _____

   _____

3. Who in your company is most likely to object or have the most difficulty with your payout option and why?

   _____

   _____

   _____

CHAPTER 6

TEACHING EMPLOYEES HOW PROFIT WORKS

EMPLOYEES *CAN* UNDERSTAND

As we've mentioned, the incentive plan shouldn't become an entitlement plan. If you get to the end of the period and pay out an incentive, but you haven't seen a value-added behavior change that led to improved performance, then you're slowly creeping toward an entitlement mentality. The thinking going on in an employee's mind is, *I can just keep doing what I've been doing, and now I get a bonus.* This isn't the mindset we're looking for. You must help influence changed behavior so that you see, and your employees feel, they've *earned* the incentive pool they're sharing. This creates a sense of pride and accomplishment.

The plan must be self-funded. For this to be true, it's your responsibility as owners and leaders to provide employees with the tools, training, leadership, and management for them to become active participants in funding the plan. A large part of this is providing them with context. This chapter will provide you with ideas for teaching your employees about profit: what it is, how it is created, and how they can drive improvements in profit to fund their incentive plan.

As you know, there are typically three financial statements in business (the income statement, the cash flow statement, and the balance sheet). Regardless of which design you've chosen, your incentive plan is most likely based on a number found on the income statement. Therefore, it's important to help them understand what a simple income statement is and how the incentive pool is created.

Whether you believe that your employees can understand an income statement, or you don't, you're right. For the incentive philosophy we describe to work, you must believe your employees can understand this at a high level. In a recent client session, we ventured into a conversation about sharing financial information with employees and how much transparency is enough. Our client said, "My employees don't give a @#%*! about financials." This mindset is what you must discard.

In our experience working with thousands of employees, we've found this isn't true. Employees *do* care! It does take some effort, discipline, structure, and intention, and you have to try. You may be shocked at how interested they are and how grateful they are that you care enough to teach and share this information. Keep in mind, they've never been taught this in school, so it will be all new to them.

> **Whether you believe that your employees can understand an income statement, or you don't, you're right.**

We had a client in Texas ask, "What if one of my employees leaves, goes to a competitor, and shares our profit numbers?" Our reply was, "So what?" Your competitors generally know the industry-standard profit percentages. If you're above industry averages, they'll be envious and curious. But your competitor can't easily mimic what makes you unique. It's no small task to copy your differentiators, your proven process and your culture.

See the transparency continuum below: on one end is a completely closed-book business, where the cards are held close to the chest and no information is shared with the employees. Toward the center, limited information is shared. Toward the right is an open-book organization. Companies find themselves all along this spectrum, of course.

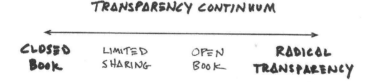

We've only encountered a handful of companies on the far right that share salaries and other personal information. We find radical transparency like that to be overkill, perhaps even a little crazy. That aside, you have to find your place on that transparency continuum, ideally just to the right of your comfort zone.

On average, in our experience, most employees believe that profit is 30-50% of revenues (or they confuse it with gross margin). What's the problem if your employees think this? For one thing, they may not say *we* make a 50% profit. They may say *you*, the owner, make a 50% profit. So, it can pit the workforce against you, promoting an Us vs. Them mentality.

Second, if they think the company is making a ton of money, they may not work as hard to eliminate operational inefficiencies, reduce waste, and offer ideas for growth. They may figure the company is making enough money, and think, *we'll just do our jobs*.

Finally, this belief leads to entitlement and disgruntlement. "How come I'm not being paid more? They can afford it." Or, "Why should I care if we lose a customer because of poor service?" Or, "Why should I care if there is trash outside the office? They can afford a cleaning crew."

Nature abhors a vacuum. When people don't know something, they make assumptions; those assumptions are usually wrong. If you believe this, then you as a business owner or executive have a choice: don't share any information with your employees and your people will think what they think. Or, share some financial information with your employees and teach them to own and drive those numbers for the benefit of your organization, themselves, and to fund the incentive plan.

This message, that the plan is theirs, is critical to beginning the shift from an entitlement plan to an earned compensation plan.

Employees should be taught to recognize that they pull levers each day that impact their incentive plan, both positively and negatively. This message, that the plan is theirs, is critical to beginning the shift from an entitlement plan to an earned compensation plan. It plants the seeds for an independence mindset and teaches them that they control their future.

Profit Works as a Return on Investment (ROI)

Before introducing a simple income statement, it's helpful to set the stage for why you're even talking about it. From a basic economic education standpoint, we all know that a business is an investment. Investors invest in things to gain a return on an investment. If there's no return, they won't take the risk or invest their money.

This basic truth about capitalism, our economic system, is helpful for your employees to understand. Whether they know it or not, your employees are capitalists every day. Your employees are investors as well (via their 401(k), home ownership, automobile, etc.). It's critical to begin to pull them into this reality because, in our experience, many employees believe investing is only something business owners and Wall Street-types do.

Where do investment returns come from? You need to teach your employees that all returns come from profit. With this fact established, you can begin to help your employees understand that profit is *critical* to influencing decisions. As participants in the incentive plan, they have a vested interest in maximizing their returns through payouts. By teaching basic economic literacy, you're trying to strengthen the link between your employees' daily activities (the things they do and decide every day) and their potential payouts via the incentive plan.

To ensure employees understand what returns are, it is helpful to introduce the terms *risk*, *return*, and *liquidity*, and discuss their interrelationship. In a group setting, ask your employees to provide definitions, and identify keywords related to risk, return, and liquidity. When discussing risk, you should hear words like uncertainty, outcome, chance, scary, win, lose, etc. They need to understand that risk is simply the chance of loss.

Once it's clear they understand the meaning of risk, do the same for returns. Talk about returns in terms of a percentage. Ask for examples from your employees that demonstrate the concept. For example, since its inception through 2019, the S&P 500 has returned a historic annualized average return on investment of around 10%. Explain that an expected return isn't a guaranteed return.

Once it's clear there's understanding around risk and return, ask if anyone can define the term liquidity. Explain that liquidity is how easy it is to

Explain that an expected return isn't a guaranteed return.

convert something into cash. Show them a dollar bill and explain that the dollar bill is the most liquid form of value because it's already cash you can spend. Give examples of other less liquid forms of value (gold, stocks, bonds, mutual funds, a house, etc.). Money invested in property or a new business might be difficult to convert into cash and thus isn't very liquid.

Ask your employees where all returns come from. Explain that in every instance, investment returns are always generated from somebody's profits, whether it's a savings account at a bank earning interest as a return, or a new business venture delivering a profit. Profit is always the thing that generates the returns. If the institution or company that's involved isn't making a profit, it can't pay the dividends on stocks, it can't pay the interest on bonds, and it can't pay the interest on a savings account. Profitability is the only source of these returns; it is that simple. Explain that for now, you want them to understand the definition of profit: what it is, where it comes from, and how they can affect it.

From here, teaching your employees about the income statement becomes a natural next step.

For a deeper dive into alternative activities to teach your employees about risk, return, and liquidity, visit profitworksllc.com.

4 Ways to Teach Revenue, Expenses, and Profit

This section will give you four ways to introduce a simple income statement to employees so they understand how everything is calculated (e.g., revenue, variable costs, fixed costs, profit). More importantly, this will teach them how they impact profit and as a result, how they impact their incentive plan. Four ideas we will describe are:

1. Introduce a simple income statement.

2. Compare business finance to personal finance.

3. Use a dollar-based income statement.

4. Illustrate using the 100 pennies exercise.

Keep these three important goals in mind when implementing any of these methods:

1. Help your employees understand what profit is, where it is found on the income statement, and how and why we use it to keep score.

2. Help your employees understand the difference between profit and cash; you'll need to emphasize that you are not going to borrow money to pay an incentive.

3. Help your employees understand that by providing this information, you're providing them with simple tools to become active participants in finding the money to fund their plan.

Introduce a Simple Income Statement

This section will help you explain financial concepts in terms that are easy for your employees to understand. Develop a simplified income statement as shown in the graphic below. We've provided several easy questions (and some answers, too). Use these to introduce the basic categories on a simplified income statement:

1. Q: "Can someone guess the definition of an income statement for us?" A: An income statement shows the amount of sales, costs, and profit of a business over a given period of time.

2. Q: "Why is the income statement important?" A: An owner certainly needs to understand the financial health of their investment. The company produces the income statement monthly, quarterly, and annually to monitor the company's financial health so the leaders always know the score. Additionally, when *everyone* in a company understands the financial health of the company, the potential for improvement is exponential.

3. Q: "What's meant by expenses or costs, and what are some examples from our company?" A: Labor, material, rent, insurance, etc.

4. Q: "Can someone define profit?" A: In simple terms, profit is what's left of the sales after all the fixed and variable expenses have been paid.

5. Q: "What would you guess profits are at our company as a percentage of sales?" In other words, thinking of all of the money your company takes in from sales, what percent of that is left over after all the expenses are paid? This is an amazingly interesting question for your employees, and we suggest you ask them to write their guesses down, and that you'll be sharing the answer shortly. Perhaps add a little reward for the person whose guess is closest.

6. Q: "Which has more of an impact on profit: increasing sales or decreasing costs?" This question often leads to

a powerful discussion. If your company has 5% profit after all the expenses have been paid and you cut costs by $1.00, the full dollar drops to the bottom line. If you wanted to put a dollar to the bottom line by increasing sales in this company, you'd have to increase sales by $20.00 (because $1.00 is 5% of $20.00). The general lesson is true, although the specifics could be argued. We're not saying don't increase sales, of course! We're trying to teach that we need to do both, and that reducing costs generally has the largest initial impact in the shortest amount of time.

	20XX	%
TOTAL SALES		
COST OF SALES		
GROSS PROFIT		
OPERATING EXPENSES		
PROFIT BEFORE TAX		

As you walk down the income statement, define the various cost areas (cost of sales, operating expenses, etc.). Ask your employees to guess what expenses are in each line. Help your team differentiate between the cost of goods sold and the operating expenses and give some examples from your company.

Now that your employees have seen the basic categories on a simplified income statement, you want them to determine how that applies to your company specifically. Instead of asking them to guess the exact dollar figures for each line of the income statement, we suggest asking them to guess what percentage of sales each line might be. An effective way to do this is to introduce the dollar-based income statement described below.

Here are some additional questions you might ask to make the income statement come alive:

- What is our company's fiscal year, and what does that mean?

- What time period does this income statement represent?

- What do the percentages mean?

- What has to happen for the rest of this fiscal year to be profitable and to fund the incentive plan?

- What effect does adding an extra employee have on the income statement?

- What effect does a loss have on the shareholders?

- What effect does a loss have on the employees?

COMPARE BUSINESS FINANCE TO PERSONAL FINANCE

A second effective way to introduce the income statement to your employees is to compare business finance to personal finance. You can teach that an employee's paycheck (income) is similar to your company's sales.

Then ask, "At home, what are some costs you have?" You will hear things like rent/mortgage, phone, electric, car, food, kids' education, and so forth. Teach that you subtract these costs from your paycheck to get to your own personal "profit" number. Some employees will half joke that their number is negative.

At home, if you aren't happy with your individual profit number, you can reduce costs by dropping cable TV, eating out less often, changing cell phone plans, shopping at a less expensive grocery store, closely managing the thermostat, etc. You can also increase your paycheck, the top line number, by getting a raise, an incentive payout, or a promotion. How do you do this at our company? You add more value. You can learn new skills, you grow, and you invest in yourself.

These are certainly very powerful conversations, and, from our experience, they create powerful moments for your employees. Psychologically, we're respecting our employees by drawing them into the world of finance in a low risk, non-threatening way. There's an element of appreciation we've heard from employees when companies go down this path. They get excited to change things for themselves at home. They hadn't thought of themselves as owners of their future. In many examples, they begin to move from a reactive, victim mentality, to a creative, ownership mentality.

Use a Dollar-Based Income Statement

With the dollar-based income statement exercise, boil the income statement down to its essential lines: sales, cost of sales, gross profit, operating expenses, and profit as described above. Show $1.00 at the top, next to sales, and 100% next to that, and then apply your true percentages. You can use numbers from the current year, last quarter, last year, whatever, to make the example.

	20xx	%
TOTAL SALES	$1.00	100%
COST OF SALES	$0.65	65%
GROSS PROFIT	$0.35	35%
OPERATING EXPENSES	$0.30	30%
PROFIT BEFORE TAX	$0.05	5%

You're trying to show them how the company gets to profit from sales. This is especially important if your incentive plan is designed based on a share of profits. Once they have this context, you can facilitate a group activity to have the employees discuss ways to reduce the cost of sales, increase profitable sales, increase operational efficiencies, reduce operating expenses, etc., and drive more dollars to the bottom line, thereby funding their incentive plan.

After a few quarters, a fun idea is to hand out a blank income statement to your employees, and in small groups, ask them to fill in the numbers for the last quarter using their best guesses. Have fun with this, promoting competition among the groups and giving out prizes for the group whose guesses are closest to the actual numbers. As you get to the bottom line, talk about and compare their guesses with the actual figures.

Illustrate Using the 100 Pennies Exercise

The 100 pennies analogy works well because of its visual impact. Lay out 100 pennies on a table (if you have a large group, stream to video so everyone can see easily). Explain that these 100 pennies represent sales. Then, ask someone to come forward and set aside the number of pennies representing the cost of sales (usually labor and materials). If you can use a product or service of your own as an example, even better. Describe specifically these are the costs that are *directly* associated with your sales (vs. indirect costs). What's remaining is gross profit, which is a critical number for most businesses.

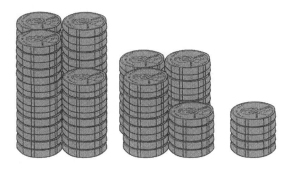

From there, ask someone else to subtract the pennies representing operating expenses (fixed costs) from the gross profit pennies. Explain that these are indirect costs that the company has to pay every month, whether you have sales or not. Examples are salaries, insurance, healthcare, rent, and so forth. What's left are your profit pennies. We suggest avoiding the use of terms like EBIT, EBITDA, net income, net operating income, etc.

Talk about how your company uses profit. As we discussed earlier, profit is used to provide a return on investment for those who've taken the risk. Profits are also used to reinvest in the business, buy new equipment, invest in new technology, provide raises, pay taxes, and pay down debt. Discuss the fact that profit is also the number from which their incentive pool is created.

In the "Show Me the Money" group activity described below, we'll discuss how to lead a group activity to have your employees talk about how they can drive more pennies toward the pile from which their incentive pool is created.

"Show Me the Money" Group Activity

Now that you've shared the basic layout of an income statement and have shown everyone where profit "lives" on your income statement, you have an opportunity to tap into their brains and ask them to contribute their ideas for moving the numbers in the right direction. Moving the numbers on the income statement in a positive way not only helps the owners of the business improve their potential return on investment, but it also drives more dollars to the bottom line, which increases the pool of money contained in a profit-based designed incentive plan. It's truly a win-win. At the same time, by going down this more inclusive and transparent path, you're building trust and gradually shifting your culture to one that contains a more engaged team.

To kick-off "Show Me the Money:"

1. Form groups of four to five employees and explain to them that you're going to discuss ways to increase the dollars in the incentive pool.

2. Ask each group to select one person to be the scribe for that group. They will take notes on the ideas.

3. In their groups, ask them to discuss one or more of the following questions:

   o Where is the money leaking out through "holes in the bucket"?

   o What kinds of headaches do you not look forward to when you're coming to work?

- ○ What kinds of topics do you discuss at the water cooler?

- ○ What inefficiencies and waste do you see in your area of the company?

- ○ What's broken in our company?

- ○ What are we doing that is stupid? What pisses you off here?

- ○ What processes do we have that slow you down?

4. Bring the large group together and have each group report. Write their answers on a visible whiteboard or flipchart. Make this interactive and have some fun. Expand on the ideas as the groups report.

5. Ask your employees how much additional profit those ideas could generate. Tie those guesses back to the impact on their incentive plan.

Example of how it might go: At a furniture retailer in Wisconsin, we did this exercise. Here was the conversation, which floored the CEO:

> Employee: "We could fix the hole in the roof of warehouse number 4. Every time it rains or snows, water gets in and damages furniture."

> CEO: "How much damage?"

> Employee: "About $250,000 a year."

> CEO: "But that's a $5,000 fix!"

It's important to note that one of the first ideas employees might have is training. You should ask them to be specific and to give real examples. Explain that training is a cost as well as an investment. Ask, "What specific training is needed?" and "How will it increase profits and contribute to our incentive plan?" You'll need to do the same when someone says "communication."

To maximize the effectiveness of the *Show Me the Money* group activity, shift their conversation slightly to focus on growth and new opportunities. Here are a few questions you can ask to set up the exercise:

- What new ideas do you have that would help our company grow?

- What new products or services should we consider that would help our company grow?

- What new investments should we consider that would help our company grow?

- What new technologies should we consider that would help our company grow?

An enormous benefit to doing these types of exercises is that they help the employees understand that *they* affect and change the numbers on the income statement every day through their actions and decisions. The group exercises and discussion that ensue reinforce the link between their activities and the potential payouts in the incentive plan. It should also generate ideas for Challenge Rocks (See Tension Tool 2 in Chapter 7).

Cash Caveat

We've discussed that we must have cash to pay out an incentive and that we aren't going to borrow money to pay our incentive. As we discussed in earlier chapters, in any of the designs, you can certainly add a cash gatekeeper if cash flow has historically been an issue. When setting the context for the plan, be sure to emphasize the difference between cash and profit.

In its simplest terms, the difference is *timing*. When we make a sale, it doesn't mean we have the cash; there are payment terms in most cases that create a timing gap between when we invoice and when we collect. Help your employees understand that your team must manage that timing to your benefit. Give them an example of the average time it takes you to collect cash and explain that you're still paying for things like salaries and rent during this time.

If you have a few customers that stretch out payment terms, this is a great time to help everyone understand this. Also, explain that when you borrow money to cover cash gaps, you have a new cost called "interest expense" on the income statement, and, as a new expense, this obligation reduces the size of their incentive pool. So, we want to minimize and certainly control how often we borrow money.

Key Takeaways

- To be successful educating non-financial people about finance, you must believe that your employees have the capacity to understand a simple income statement.

- Profit works as a return on investment for investors.

- Simplify the income statement to most effectively teach it to your employees.

- To teach the income statement to your employees, consider using a simplified income statement, comparing business finance to personal finance, using a dollar-based income statement, and/or using the 100 pennies exercise.

- Through interactive discussion, help your employees understand the link between their daily activities and the profit line on the income statement.

- Facilitate a "Show Me the Money" group activity to engage your employees in a discussion of improvements they can make that would contribute to an increase in potential incentive plan payouts.

THINKING QUESTIONS

1. Do you believe your employees can understand the basics of revenue, expenses, and profit?

    _____

    _____

    _____

2. Where does your company sit today on the transparency continuum?

    _____

    _____

    _____

3. Now move further to the right; what would be the risks?

    _____

    _____

    _____

4. What would be the benefits to moving further to the right?

    _____

    _____

    _____

5. Which teaching exercises in this chapter appeal to you the most? What's your next step?

_____

_____

_____

Chapter 7

Tools to Create Just Enough Tension

Tension Tool 1: Scorecards and Measurables

As a growth-minded entrepreneur, you have undoubtedly been exposed to and perhaps used measurables, scorecards, dashboards, and other data management tools to drive your business. In our experience, everyone must have 1-3 numbers or measurables to drive accountability and responsibility, and it is a huge advantage to teach employees that these numbers are their key levers toward creating a self-funded incentive plan.

For one of our clients, this number was utilization, i.e., how many hours they billed the clients each week versus how many hours they worked. For another client, it was revenue per driver per day and deliveries per day. At another, it was sales calls per day and quoted dollars. This may seem daunting at first, but once you get your employees more involved, you'll find that having your employees help track and report measurables is actually very easy and impactful. It also puts the onus on them, helping them buy in more to the process, and reinforcing the tie between their activities and their incentive plan.

Track measurables on a scorecard on a weekly basis. Also, tie each measurable to someone's name. When you have a name on the scorecard, you also have accountability. Reviewing the scorecard with frequency and accountability adds positive tension to your workforce. As you cascade the measurables throughout your company, you include everyone in this tension and accountability.

Note: you don't have to do this for everyone at the same time. Take it in manageable, bite-sized chunks.

SALES DEPARTMENT SCORECARD							
WHO	MEASURABLE	GOAL	20-Jun	27-Jun	4-Jul	11-Jul	18-Jul
ALEJANDRO	# NEW LEADS						
MICHELE	# APPTS. HELD						
MICHELE	$ WON						
FLOYD	# APPTS. HELD						
FLOYD	$ WON						

In *The Truth About Employee Engagement*, Patrick Lencioni talks about immeasurability as one of the key signs of a miserable job. If an employee doesn't know how they did at the end of the day, week, or quarter, he says, it makes them feel more isolated, less relevant, and less tied to the company's vision.

Tension Tool 2: Challenge Rocks (Gamifying Rocks)

If you're running on EOS, you're familiar with and use Rocks as a discipline. Rocks are measurable 90-day priorities used not only by leadership team members but also by employees. Teams use this tool to keep a key priority on track with discipline and accountability.

An extension of a Rock that adds tension, attention, and fun is called a Challenge Rock, which is a game focused on improving an important number. A Challenge Rock is typically 90 days long and can be departmental or company-wide, depending on what measurable you're focused on improving. There are 6 steps to designing a Challenge Rock:

1. **Measurable**: Select the measurable and the Challenge Rock goal (e.g., reduce scrap from X to Y; improve utilization from C to D; talk to Z new prospects a week). Many times, the measurable the employees pick for a Challenge Rock is one that they identified in the *Show Me the Money* exercise. This is important because when employees weigh in, they buy in. If the targeted measurable is their idea, they are often more engaged in driving improvement.

2. **Benefits**: List the benefits of hitting the goal. Examples will include cost-reduction impact, better on-time delivery, improving the XYZ process, etc. Include any investments required to illustrate the importance of ROI. Ask "How does this help us achieve our goals? How will this help fund our incentive plan?"

3. **Who**: List who is leading the Challenge Rock, who else needs to be involved, and if an executive sponsor is required. An executive sponsor helps the team by removing obstacles and barriers and helps in obtaining approval for large expenditures.

4. **What**: Identify what needs to happen and what actions you will take to hit your Challenge Rock goal. These may not all be known at the beginning and that is okay. Don't get too caught up in creating a detailed project plan. This may involve some deeper discussion, brainstorming, and perhaps even establishing a *tiger team* (a term used for a team of specialists formed to work on a specific goal).

5. **Future Date**: Establish the Challenge Rock due date, typically 90 days away. The timeframe should be long enough to allow for an impact on the company, but not so long as to cause people to lose interest in the game. It is not uncommon that all the actions are completed in the first 90 days and it takes another 90 days to measure the impact. However, don't celebrate until the goal has been met.

6. **If We Win**: Give the Challenge Rock a fun title and create a company-wide celebration if the Challenge Rock is accomplished (e.g., a big pizza party, escape room, axe throwing, etc.).

For example, a 90-day Rock for one of our clients was to "Close $1 million in new business." This is a SMART Rock (specific, measurable, attainable, realistic, and timely). The team members knew what "done" would look like when the

Rock was complete, and it became a great candidate for a Challenge Rock. The sales team worked together on the six steps listed above and in about 15 minutes, developed milestones of small potential wins throughout the quarter. They designed a simple and fun visual tracking scoreboard with a large elephant on it and gave it a fun name: "Big Game Hunting." At the end of the 90-day period, when they surpassed the $1 million target, they celebrated with a day at the zoo with everyone from the company and their families.

Challenge Rocks are great because they blend a financial focus with a culture of participation and fun. When you teach Challenge Rocks to your employees, and they really embrace the tool, you will begin to see how the incentive plan becomes more than just an extrinsic motivator.

There is real intrinsic value to your employees, not only because the plan contributes incremental dollars to their incentive payouts, but also because it provides a team win.

The psychology behind establishing a Challenge Rock is to arm your employees with another tool, ideally a fun one, to help them actively participate in funding their incentive plan. It also strengthens the link between their daily efforts and their potential payout in the incentive plan.

It's fun when you win! Be sure to celebrate as a company, even if it's just one department that has won their Challenge Rock. The recognition and the praise that the winning employees feel goes a long way. It's good practice to start with an easy Challenge Rock first to get some early success and momentum.

One caution! Be sure the potential payback from successfully completing a Challenge Rock more than covers any investments in equipment, process changes you may have to make, and the celebration.

CHALLENGE ROCK

Challenge Title: _____

📊 Measurable

Select the measurable you're gamifying, and the Challenge Rock goal.

Examples:

- Improve close rate from X to Y

- Improve utilization from C to D

💵 Benefits

List the benefits of hitting the goal, and how it contributes to the incentive pool.

Examples:

- Reduce cost

- Reduce touchpoints leading to increased customer satisfaction

- Improved ABC Process

👤 Who

Who is leading the Challenge Rock?

Who else needs to be involved?

Is there an executive sponsor?

❓ What

Identify what needs to happen and what actions you will take to hit your Challenge Rock goal.

This may involve deeper discussion and brainstorming as a team, and you may not know all the steps when you begin – just start making progress!

📅 Future Date

Establish the due date – typically 90 days.

🎉 If We Win...

Create a company-wide celebration if you hit the Challenge Rock goal.

At the top of this worksheet – add a fun title!

Tension Tool 3: Meeting Discipline

Quarterly Meetings: Frequent updates for your employees are critical to the success of your incentive plan. We suggest a Quarterly State of the Company Address (SOCA). The basic agenda is: past, present, and future. Or, where we've been, where we are, and where we're going.

A simple way to populate what information you're going to share in each meeting is to brainstorm with your leadership team a few weeks ahead of time. What updates do we need to provide? Focus your brainstorming around topics such as people, processes, technology, and financials. Sometime during this update, let everyone know where the company is with the incentive plan (the score of the game).

Be sure to share both good and bad news, as this builds trust and helps the team feel like their leadership team has the wheel and knows what's going on. You can talk about various Challenge Rocks taking place, success stories, improvements, pictures, employee and client stories of impact, investments, and more. No strict rules here; it's key that you're communicating and doing so in a methodical, structured way.

Although we suggest quarterly company updates, more frequent updates will never hurt. Some of our clients have monthly 15-minute updates. It can be helpful to align the frequency of your updates with the payout frequency you've established. When you tie your incentive plan updates into the company vision, you help link your employees' daily efforts with your longer-term vision.

With these updates, everyone knows what they need to do, what numbers they need to drive, and how you're doing as a company. You're moving toward one company with one vision. In our experience, people need to hear something seven times for them to hear it for the first time. Communication is an intentional investment of time. You'll have to schedule and prepare for these meetings and update your team on how you're doing. This takes time. Be prepared. Be intentional.

Weekly Meetings: In addition to quarterly company-wide meetings, a regular weekly meeting discipline is important to identify and solve short-term issues, keep the circles connected on key priorities, and advance teamwork toward funding the incentive plan.

Meetings are not a waste of time; it's what many teams do in meetings that can be a waste of time. Whether these are weekly leadership team meetings (typically 90 minutes) or daily stand-ups with departmental teams, the general rule for time management is:

- One-third of the time is spent identifying issues and providing updates on important initiatives.

- Two-thirds of the time is spent making progress on the most important issues or off-track items.

These meetings are not gripe sessions; they are issues-solving sessions. You must maintain discipline in holding these meetings. The only reasons for missing a meeting are death and vacation. Correcting off-track items in these meetings is an essential discipline to making progress toward funding the incentive plan.

More details on conducting these meetings can be found in the books *Traction* and *What the Heck is EOS?*, listed in Appendix D.

KEY TAKEAWAYS

- The use of scorecards and measurables throughout your company is a critical tension tool to drive more accountability and discipline.

- Challenge Rocks are effective 90-day games that blend a financial focus with a culture of participation and fun.

- Frequent company updates are important so you can tell everyone what the score is, over-communicate with your employees, and reinforce for everyone the tie between their daily actions and the payout potential in their incentive plan.

- Regular weekly meetings and daily stand-ups are great practices to introduce into your culture to improve communication, address issues quickly, and reinforce the connection between solving off-track items and their impact on the incentive plan.

THINKING QUESTIONS

1. Do you have access to timely and accurate financial information?

   _____

   _____

   _____

2. Do you have scorecards and measurables throughout your company? If so, are they working to help your teams make better and faster decisions?

   _____

   _____

   _____

3. What are three initiatives you can think of that might be great 90-day Challenge Rocks for your employees to implement?

   _____

   _____

   _____

4. Do you have regular weekly meetings? If so, how might you make them more effective?

_____

_____

_____

5. Do you have regular company-wide meetings that allow you to communicate with everyone in the company? How often are they, and what benefits are you seeing?

_____

_____

_____

6. What additional information might you want to share in those company-wide meetings?

_____

_____

_____

Chapter 8

What's Next

To the degree the message in this book resonates with you, and you decide to implement some of our suggestions, we'd love for you to share your experiences and questions with us.

When you run your company purely on an operating system, your vision is inspiring, it's communicated often, and the intentional tension tools are embedded deep into your organization. When you run your company on an operating system *and* you have a simple incentive plan in place, you'll have the confidence to accelerate toward your goals, knowing that every one of your employees is equipped, has your company's best interest in mind, and has the knowledge that we *all* win when the company wins.

Together, you and your team create and execute on your vision, and together, you *earn* that pride of accomplishment, as well as a little extra profit in your pockets.

**For more information and resources,
visit us at ProfitWorksLLC.com**

APPENDIX A

MINDSET SCORECARD

Mindsets	1	2	3	4	5	6
1 Transparency	You believe that only the owners should know about the financials of the company. They're too overwhelming as it is.			You're open to sharing financial information with people, but are worried they won't understand it or that they might share it elsewhere.		
2 Teamwork	You don't have time to worry about everyone else. It's every man for himself. People will earn based on their individual effort.			You recognize great teamwork is possible, but only with lots of work. You're not sure you have the right leaders to inspire strong teamwork.		
3 Growth	You worked hard to get where you are and you aren't ready to share profits with people who don't own the business or put in as much work.			You want to grow and have tried a lot of things, but nothing seems to be working. Growth just doesn't happen here. You can't figure it out.		
4 People Matter	You know people are important: they drive profits and provide a return on investment for the company, but investing in them seems fruitless.			You know people are your best asset. You know they have the capacity to understand how profit works, but you need tools to help them.		
5 Operating System Discipline	You know everyone wears lots of hats and pitches in to do what needs to be done. You all work really hard and use a lot of common sense.			You've tried so many systems, but are frustrated with your people, your profits and a lack of control over your business. Nothing sticks.		
6 Data Discipline	Your financials and data are pretty disorganized and outdated. Sometimes you spend money in a reactionary way or on frivolous things.			You have decent, somewhat organized financials; you study the data and publish a budget every year, but you rarely stick to it.		
7 Earning	You don't think incentive plans change behavior permanently, but people feel they deserve them. A fair salary should be motivation enough.			You know incentive plans can change employee behavior, but the design & administration are complex and time consuming. They just fizzle out.		
8 Ownership	If people work hard, they deserve a bonus & you'll give them one. You pay fairly, give regular raises, often tied to tenure.			You pay fairly & try performance-based incentives. When people don't hit goals, you may pay out anyway, even when you haven't made money.		
Scorecard	⇒	⇒	⇒	⇒	⇒	⇒

H.SCB.DS.1000

Mindset Scorecard

Name:	Date:					A	B
7	**8**	**9**	**10**	**11**	**12**		
You don't think employees need to see the financials; they just need a target to hit. People only care about money & they need to do their jobs.			You know that when people have good information, they make better, more informed decisions. It's important that the company is transparent.				
You have effective teams and teamwork is fine. Team health stuff is silly; it would be easier if people just showed up and did their work.			You know effective teamwork is key to successful business. When teams achieve, there's a culture of pride, celebration, confidence and growth.				
Your business is stable: generating predictable cash flow allowing owner distributions/reinvestment. You don't want to disrupt your cash cow with changes.			You have a Growth Mindset; when the company wins, you all win. As you include people, they see growth. If you're not growing, you're dying.				
You pay people for their time and contribution: a transaction that works for all. If someone's not happy about it, they can work elsewhere.			You care deeply about people & teach them how to get everything they want out of life. You touch the lives of many people through your work.				
You track data: measure your people. They know what to do & there are performance measuring systems in place. You're organized & efficient.			A company can't improve or see growth using multiple operating systems, so you run one OS; it's the foundation for a great incentive plan.				
You have timely and accurate financial information and measure anything that can be measured. Your financials are detailed and complex.			You have timely, accurate data; track leading & lagging measurables at all levels. Scorecards are visible & teams use data to make decisions.				
You have incentive plans in place and employees know how to earn bonuses. You follow industry best practices & talk about it at year's end.			You experiment with ways to motivate. You seek best practices & look for new solutions. When you win as a team, you reward & celebrate together.				
It's at the discretion of the management team to decide who gets what at the end of each year. You're not giving up that control.			You believe in a simple, transparent, motivating incentive plan where everyone has control over their own earning ability.				

➡ ➡ ➡ ➡ ➡ ➡ ➡ ➡

Appendix B

Sales Departments and Incentive Plans

A client in New England imported manufactured goods from the Far East and had a problem. The Sales team viewed the Engineering department as the "anti-sales, delay everything" department. Engineering viewed Sales as "those guys who play golf, spend a lot of money on dinners, and never give us the information we need." They would barely speak to each other. We're sure this was a unique situation never experienced at any other firm.

Everyone's incentive was tied to company profits with a kicker for the salespeople based on how much they sold. We got these groups in the same room to work on Challenge Rocks. They agreed on the information engineering needed from sales and designed a simple form to communicate that information. Engineering committed to standard turn-around times on projects. They even implemented an escalation process between the managers of each department.

The result: revenue increased from $55 million to $90+ million in two years, and profit increased exponentially.

Because this book is about incentive plans, it makes sense to talk briefly about sales departments and how they tie into a company-wide incentive plan. Incentive plans for salespeople can be challenging and we include this section not as the end-all-be-all on sales incentives (there are plenty of books on that), but instead, to give you a little context and provoke a few thoughts.

There is no such thing as a perfect sales incentive plan. As with all incentive plans, the key is to keep it simple and incentivize the behavior you want from your team. Below, we'll describe three sales incentive design options to get you thinking. However you design your sales incentive plan, we suggest you include the sales team in the company-wide incentive plan. It sends a strong message about acting as one team and minimizes the isolation that teams often feel.

We suggest you include the sales team in the company-wide incentive plan.

True sales incentives are "Me Comp," not "We Comp," and as you'd expect, these are not the same. Typically, salespeople participate in the company incentive plan as well as their sales incentive plan. We'll address this at the end of this section. We've also seen sales teams with 50% of their incentive based on how they do individually and 50% based on how the team or firm performs. Last, we use the word *incentive,* although most salespeople would call this a commission. Keep in mind these options are towards the ends of the spectrum, and there are a lot of options in between.

SALES COMP. SPECTRUM

HIGH BASE /
LOW INCENTIVE

LOW BASE /
HIGH INCENTIVE

HIGH BASE SALARY/LOWER SALES INCENTIVE

As a rough guide, this approach means that 80% of compensation is salary and 20% is based on sales generated. This is common when there are fewer transactions or when you have a long sales cycle. It's also used when salespeople don't have to do a lot of selling and are really order takers or account managers.

This type of structure is also often used with new product offerings or when a company is entering a new market where there aren't many established relationships. Often, this requires more of a business development salesperson. This approach can also be used in a new company, when you're trying to attract talent, or with new salespeople to allow them a ramp-up period before lowering their base and increasing their commission.

Top Six Use Cases:

- Account managers

- Entering new markets

- New company with a lot of unknowns

- Attracting talent

- Launching new products

- Team of "farmers" not "hunters"

Low Base Salary/Higher Incentive

The alternative is a low base salary with a higher incentive plan, meaning roughly 20% salary and 80% commission. This works very well in highly transactional businesses or where the company is generating quality leads for salespeople, and all sales needs to do is close the business. Notice we said *quality* leads. Nothing is more frustrating than trying to close crappy leads when your paycheck is based on this model.

This can also be effective when salespeople can close the sale and then hand the customer off to account management or operations. Once the sale is closed, the salespeople aren't responsible for maintaining the account day-to-day or delivering the product or service.

Top Six Use Cases:

- High volume of transactions

- Quality leads provided to salespeople

- Salespeople can hand off closed sales to others for execution

- Team of "hunters" not "farmers"

- Salary is a "draw"

- Salespeople make it or leave (think real estate, wealth management, or automobile sales)

An Unusual Option

Dan Pink's July 2012 article from *Harvard Business Review* called "A Radical Prescription for Sales" shares some interesting data about motivation as it relates to sales compensation. In a counterintuitive conclusion, he describes several situations wherein business owners abandoned sales incentives. Instead, these owners established higher base salaries and pulled the salespeople into the company's incentive plan. With this approach, the results consistently demonstrated a sales increase with no change in the cost of sales.

One of our clients implemented this option with similar results. His biggest concern was losing his best salespeople, and he did lose one top salesperson. But the person who left was more me-focused than we-focused. When you have core values misalignment like this, dropping a cultural misfit or two is a good change. It's multiplication by subtraction. The newly amplified message of teamwork and fighting together for the greater good shifted the company's culture. Peer-to-peer accountability increased. New account information from the field was more accurate and complete as team members didn't want to let each other down.

Whether from the new-found team unity and collaboration, a level playing field and a sense of fairness, salespeople feeling less isolated, or, perhaps, some combination of these, the results speak for themselves. Success here truly depends on the type of culture you're trying to create. You get what you reward: rugged individualism or a true team. Neither is right nor wrong. In fact, these can be not only culture-specific, but also industry-specific.

Any incentive plan does not excuse you from being a great leader and exceptional manager.

A note of caution: this approach may sound great (or not) but as with all sales teams, it will still require management and leadership.

To be clear, we're not advocating any of these specific approaches. We only hope that this gets you thinking about your approach and that you consider including the sales team in the company incentive plan.

Appendix C

Incentive Plans in Scary Times

The black swan theory was developed by Nassim Nicholas Taleb and, according to Wikipedia, "refers to unexpected events of large magnitude and consequence and their dominant role in history." As we were completing this book, the world was punched in the face with one of these. Any scary time, such as a terrorist attack or a recession, creates uncertainty for every business.

As we've watched the consequences of this scary time unfold, we've witnessed two significant shifts: many companies are recalibrating their annual plans, and many companies have an increased number of employees who now work from home (WFH).

When your workforce is no longer visible, and when your confidence is tested on the annual goals around which you designed your incentive plan, how should you respond? There are essentially three options to consider: keep your incentive plan, modify it, or abandon it.

KEEP THE INCENTIVE PLAN

For some companies, it may make sense to keep the annual plan as-is and keep the incentive plan as it's designed. If you hit your plan, and you hit the incentive threshold, of course, you'll pay it out, but for now, tell your team they probably shouldn't count on a payout.

In this situation, you have a fantastic opportunity to lean into the positive tension tools we described in Chapter 7. You might establish a theme for the year, a visible motto, or a call-to-action to rally everyone around the required effort.

If you decide to keep your incentive plan, and at the end of the year, you don't hit the threshold, then, of course, don't pay it out. If you pay it out after missing the targets, the psychological consequence is significant, and your team won't soon forget it. They'll be thinking, *It doesn't matter if we don't hit our goals; management will pay it out anyway.* (See Mistake #2 in Chapter 3.)

As an example, the 2020 Annual EOS Conference was sold out. It was to be an in-person event in Indianapolis. Because of health restrictions, the conference team quickly pivoted to a virtual event. We ran the virtual conference on EOS, using all the EOS Tools and adapting them, speeding up our Meeting Pulse™ and decision-making. In the end, we surpassed our original goals. By *not* changing the incentive tied to the event and really leaning into the tension tools we learned in "peacetime," we achieved pride, satisfaction, exceptional teamwork, and collaboration and exceeded our financial goals, including the incentive payout.

MODIFY THE INCENTIVE PLAN

When running on EOS, we coach our clients *not* to change their annual plan after they finalize it. We want them to get used to living and dying by their predictions and to learn from their accurate *and* erroneous forecasts so they can continue to grow on their journey to becoming their best.

You might adapt this same philosophy as you consider what to do with your incentive plan during a scary time. As we mentioned above, we suggest you *not* roll out your incentive plan until you're sure it's final. If you roll out your incentive plan and then change it a short time later, you damage trust. No one likes playing a game when the rules keep changing.

Studies show that sustained uncertainty resulting from changing rules leads to stress, lower productivity, and lower levels of creative thinking. So, if *not* changing the rules of the game is the rule, then what are we supposed to do during a world crisis? Changing the rules would be the exception.

How you communicate that you're changing the rules and *why* you're changing them is the key here. As entrepreneurs, we can't rescue our team every time we miss a target (see Mistake #2 in Chapter 3). If you frequently rescue your team, you're on a path to perpetuating an entitlement mentality in your culture.

As we've discussed, the potential consequence of changing the rules to pay out an incentive is the loss of trust, confidence, and credibility as a leader. Because of these potential consequences and the potential for weakening accountability in your culture, gather your team together, and talk about the *why*. Help them understand that you're not going to do this every year. You're not going to rescue them every time you're losing the game. Help them understand that doing so would promote entitlement.

You could simply say, "Hey team, this crisis is an unprecedented event. We rarely change the rules, but we have decided to modify the incentive plan because we care about you, we care about each other, we feel it's the right thing to do, and we want to keep all of our heads in the game." Also, it's a great opportunity to tap the potential within your team for ideas to get the plan back on track.

As an example, sales on one team fell by 45% at the outset of the crisis in 2020. They quickly adjusted their targets as well as their incentive plan trigger and communicated this to their team with speed. When any crisis hits, speed is critical. The timing of this type of communication is critical. We suggest you accelerate your adaptation. We now have so many wonderful business and data mining tools to accelerate the detection and correction of errors. Right now, this team is on track to being down by only 10% as they've driven toward gains they initially didn't realize were possible.

When any crisis hits, speed is critical.

ABANDON THE INCENTIVE PLAN

A third option is to abandon the incentive plan to reflect the new reality. During a world crisis, we aren't doing elective surgery; we're in the emergency room. For some companies, the decision must be *there is no incentive plan this year*. As we suggested above, when you outline your plan, be sure to include a brief note that essentially says, "in the event of unforeseen circumstances, management reserves the right to end or modify the plan at any time."

You want your company to be here for the long term, and you may be struggling to stay alive, let alone save jobs. Having an incentive plan isn't a priority right now. You're probably thinking: *We're all fortunate to have jobs and some sense of security; that's what we should be thankful for.* It's a tough message, but that's why we need strong leaders.

What's essentially happened because of this black swan event is the original incentive goal has become unattainable (see Mistake #4 in Chapter 3). Should you decide to abandon the plan, then, to keep the team engaged and not move everyone toward a bailout and a sense of entitlement, you might consider an alternative reward as well as the implementation of a series of Challenge Rocks with fun celebrations.

One client decided to give everyone at the company a $500 cash gift as a thank you for being part of the team and for sticking with the company during this tough time. Another client decided to plan a party at the end of the year instead of paying out incentives. A third chose to provide gift cards to a local restaurant for their team members to take their spouses or families out to a nice dinner.

To be sure, these are rewards, not incentives. They're gifts. If you do decide at some point to abandon your incentive plan when a crisis or another unpredictable event occurs, you might consider ideas like these. Just be sure to communicate the *why* when you roll these out to your team.

Because events like these can happen anytime, the message in this book is more important now than ever. With more employees working from home, we've moved rapidly to a results-oriented work environment. It's no longer time-based. Leaders and employees realize they shouldn't worry about when others are taking breaks, how they're using their time, or what hours of the day they work. It's about results; it's about the data. This emphasizes the importance of scorecards and other accountability tools to provide that data. The pendulum is moving faster toward autonomy with more virtual employees, and we need to trust work from home (WFH) employees to manage their time and be accountable for their results.

Incentives during scary times are a catalyst for more frequent and better communication, motivation, and excitement as we continue to gamify the business world. We're moving to an environment where enhanced trust and employee autonomy are more the norms. In the best cultures, an incentive plan has become an effective tool for aligning employees' actions with the company's vision and ensuring results are the primary focus. Healthy, enlightened leaders understand this.

Appendix D

Recommended Reading

The Black Swan, Nassim Nicholas Taleb

The Bucket Bonus Plan, created by Steve Wilson

Drive: The Surprising Truth About What Motivates Us, Dan Pink

The Earning Advantage: 8 Tools You Need to Get Paid the Money You Want, Jill Young

The Great Game of Business, Jack Stack

Ownership Thinking, Brad Hams

The Patient Organization: Attracting, Engaging, and Empowering Team Players, Walt Brown

The Power of Open-Book Management, John Schuster and Jill Carpenter

Traction, Gino Wickman

The Truth About Employee Engagement: A Fable About Addressing the Three Root Causes of Job Misery, Patrick Lencioni

SAMPLE CHAPTER: WHAT THE HECK IS EOS?

Also available in Spanish and on Audible.com
in both English and Spanish.

WHAT THE HECK IS

EOS?

A Complete Guide for
Employees in Companies
Running on EOS

GINO WICKMAN
& TOM BOUWER

CONTENTS

INTRODUCTION

We've written this book for you because you play a critical role in your company's success and, therefore, your own—because your success and your company's are deeply linked.

Whether you are a customer service rep, accountant, field-service rep, salesperson, sales-support staff, welder, truck driver, architect, consultant, or any other role, this book was written to help you be more successful in your company—a company running on EOS (the Entrepreneurial Operating System).

So, what the heck is EOS?

CHAPTER 1

WHAT THE HECK IS EOS?

Your company is using EOS (the Entrepreneurial Operating System) as its "operating system." So, what the heck does that mean for you? Before answering that question, it's important to first understand that every company has an operating system, whether it has a name or not.

That system is the way a company organizes all of its human energy. It's the way that the people in the organization meet, solve problems, plan, prioritize, follow processes, communicate, measure, structure, clarify roles, lead, and manage.

1

It's hard to understand the operating systems of most companies because the leadership teams aren't consistent in how they do the above. This inconsistency leads to poor communication, dysfunction, and employees feeling frustrated and confused about what the priorities are. Ultimately, the company never realizes its full potential.

The reason you're reading this book is that your leadership team wants everyone in your organization to understand how EOS works, to see the value of its structure, and to help them implement it.

Why one operating system? The short answer is that everyone doing it their own way in an organization can't work. You can't have a company where everyone can set the priorities, meet the way they want to meet, and use different terminology.

If you have 50 people doing everything 50 different ways, the increased complexity leads to mass chaos. Even worse, people experience incredible confusion and frustration. Simply put, you can't build a great company on multiple operating systems—you must choose one.

For instance, at an IT services company in Atlanta, every project was managed differently because each project manager led their project their own way. When employees moved from one project to the next, they had to learn a whole new project management system with different reporting, status updates, and meeting structures. As a result, they wasted a lot of time trying to learn a new system—time that should have been spent serving clients. Due to this inconsistent approach, people grew frustrated, and the company started losing clients, employees, and money.

The truth is, a team of average people running their company on one operating system will outperform a team of high achievers, each doing it their own way, every day of the week. That is why your company needs a clearly stated operating system that everyone follows.

WHY EOS?

So, why this operating system? Because it works. More than 50,000 companies all over the world run on EOS. It's a complete, simple, and powerful operating system. It helps companies grow to achieve their vision and goals more effectively.

It also gives the employees of those companies a well-defined structure in which they can grow, feel more fulfilled in their work, and achieve their personal goals. It helps them feel more "in-the-know" about what's going on. When you understand what the priorities of the company are, it helps you play your part in achieving them.

As Kathleen Watts, an account manager at PMMC, put it, "Before EOS, I didn't have a lot of insight into the bigger picture. Communication from management was not streamlined. Now we're much more aligned as an organization, and I know what we are trying to do and how I can help."

EOS also saves time. When everyone in your organization is rowing in the same direction, you'll find that you are communicating better. EOS eliminates unhealthy and time-wasting activities due to miscommunication. Down the road, that means avoiding train wrecks that can cost your company tons of money and cause you lots of headaches.

At a Connecticut technology firm, meetings would go for hours and hours without anything ever getting resolved. The CEO said, "Once we implemented EOS, we stopped wasting time with unnecessary meetings. We're getting more done and are communicating more effectively with our employees. They've told me that as a company, we make a lot fewer mistakes and now solve problems before they become major disasters."

EOS AND YOUR LEADERSHIP TEAM

EOS is specifically designed for a 10- to 250-person entrepreneurial company that is open-minded and growth-oriented. In our experience, this is where EOS has the most impact. While it works for companies larger and smaller, this is the true sweet spot for EOS.

As a part of implementing EOS, you will notice that the leadership team of your organization goes off-site occasionally for full-day working sessions. They do this to get 100 percent in sync and on the same page with each other. When away from the office, they work hard to solve all of the high-level issues facing your company and to set quarterly priorities. This ensures that the entire organization can stay laser-focused on achieving your company vision.

Business is hard—that's reality. With constantly changing technology, competition trying to crush you, and demanding customers and clients, your leadership team has to wrestle with 136 issues at any given time. They can't succeed without great people throughout your organization. They can't do it without *you*.

EOS AND YOU

It's also important that *you* know you can't do it alone. You need a team that you can depend on and that can depend on you. If you've been thinking, "What's in it for me?" that's fair and understandable. The short answer is that EOS will help you to work more effectively, with less frustration and a clearer understanding of the connection between your efforts and the success of your company.

As one employee said, "EOS helped me really understand where I fit in the company and how I impact everyone else. We have a great team, and it is fun to work here."

You may be thinking that implementing EOS in your organization sounds rigid, will stifle creativity, and will rob you of your uniqueness. Actually, just the opposite happens. Just as a computer's operating system is an underlying framework that helps you be more productive, EOS will do the same for you and your organization. Its underlying framework will magnify your unique contribution and help you be more productive.

So now that you know why your company is implementing EOS, let's begin the journey, because that's what this is. EOS is not a project with a specific end date. Implementing EOS in your company is an ongoing, lifelong effort. Many companies have been running on EOS for more than 10 years.

To start the journey with your company, first you need to understand the big picture, which we will describe in Chapter 2. Then, in Chapters 3-7 we will share the 5 foundational tools that form the back-bone of EOS. Finally, in Chapter 8, we will share a few bonus tools that will be the icing on the cake.

THE TRACTION LIBRARY

ACKNOWLEDGMENTS

This book would not have been possible without the help, guidance, and support of many people. You've impacted our lives in many ways, and we will never be able to thank you enough.

Tom's Family, Teachers, Mentors, and Friends

John Bouwer, my father. Thank you again for the amazing lessons I have learned by watching you and sometimes even listening to you. You taught me and demonstrated values, ethics, and making hard decisions.

Marian Bouwer, my mother. Thank you for your strength and love, for understanding me, and for being patient when needed. And, for teaching me how to cook something other than Ramen Noodles.

Alex Freytag, my business partner, co-author, and world-class EOS Implementer. No words can adequately describe my gratitude. Thank you for pushing me, for helping me grow, for Clarity Trips™, and many other things that have added immeasurable value to my life. I'm looking forward to our next fun and rewarding adventures together. It has been a blast.

Becky Pearson, our amazing assistant. You do so much for me; my thanks are truly inadequate. I'm amazed you are always on top of things—even when I call you at the store. (Oh, and with 4 kids, a dog, a cat, a husband, 2+ books, the EOS Conference, etc.) You keep me focused and relatively calm. Your passion and drive for our collective success is, for me, pure delight.

My Clients. Thank you for trusting me on this journey, for taking it with me, and for laughing, crying, and approaching every session with openness and honesty (and for calling me out when needed). I learn from you every time we are together. You inspire me every day.

The Professional EOS Implementer Community™. What a wonderful group to be a part of. Your "help first" core value is apparent in every interaction I have with all of you. A special call out to the Harry Gates tribe. Thanks for your love and support, for trusting Alex and me, and for being such a special part of our "Grow or Die" approach.

My Mentors and Coaches. Alex and I frequently talk about how much influence you've had, and continue to have, in our lives. Finally, to the person who created this amazing journey—Gino Wickman. Thank you for trusting me, encouraging me, and helping me make a significant impact in the world.

Alex's Family, Teachers, Mentors, and Friends

'Appreciate', *verb*, to increase in value. We teach in this book that before any reward, there must be an increase in value. This is a guiding principle for me taught to me initially by my parents, Betsy and the late Donald A. Freytag, and reinforced through the years by so many additional people for whom I have deep respect, admiration, and gratitude. Massive appreciation, Mom and Dad. Thank you.

My coaches, mentors, bosses, clients, family members, friends, fellow entrepreneurs, and most likely a few strangers, have also contributed in one way or another to this book. I will never be able to thank you all enough for your impact on my life, my work, and this book, but here's a start.

Tom Bouwer, my co-author, my partner (business partner, that is), and a fantastic EOS Implementer. Writing this book with you was fun, another adventure for sure, and I can't thank you enough for your leadership, our friendship, and all the value we've created together.

My brothers, Don and Gavin Freytag. Thank you, guys, for being great role models for me, for blazing the trails, for calling me on my bullshit, and for taking the arrows so I could learn from all your mistakes. :) Gavin, our early work together on ProfitWorks 1.0 created such a valuable foundation for all my work today—thank you.

Becky Pearson, our fantastic assistant. Thanks for keeping me on track, for catching my spinning plates, and for allowing me to elevate to my highest and best use. For your commitment and your passion—thank you, Beck.

My family. Thank you for your unending support for my crazy ideas. Christine, my strong and beautiful wife, for taking heaps off my plate so I can focus. Alec, my reliable, focused, and intelligent first born. Sophia, my daughter who is wisdom, creativity, beauty, and ambition. Ethan, my quick-witted, warm, super-caring, last born: you guys keep me laughing and help me keep my ego in check. I love you all very much. Thank you.

My clients, a big thanks for trusting me, for laughing with me, and sometimes at me, for making the EOS journey such a fun and memorable one. We grow together. I love your passion for this pursuit and your 'grow or die' core value. We are mirrors for each other.

The Professional EOS Implementer Community and especially the Harry Gates tribe: thank you for your love, your support, and encouragement, and your open and honest talk. For trusting me and for taking a chance on Tom and me here and there. So much gratitude, appreciation, and respect on our journey together.

My past coaches, mentors and bosses: a big thank you. Tom and I recognize that we are standing on the shoulders of giants, and we can't thank you enough for giving it to us straight, for teaching us and believing in us, knowing that we had it in us before we even knew it. Gino Wickman, I feel privileged to help you put a dent in this universe. Thank you, brother.

CONTRIBUTORS AND MANUSCRIPT READERS

Alec Broadfoot, Bob Shenefelt, Chris White, Dan Sullivan, Denise Foley, Dino Signore, Don Sasse, Drew Flora, Gino Wickman, Greg Guy, Jill Young, John McMahon, John Schuster, Josh Holtzman, Larry Hart, Lynda Martin, Nathen Fox, René Boer, Sandy King, Sara Stern, Serafina Pupillo, Shannon Waller, Ted Coons, Walt Brown

ABOUT THE AUTHORS

 Tom Bouwer, co-author of *What the Heck is EOS?*, has a passion for helping people get what they want from their businesses. To fulfill that passion, he helps entrepreneurs and their leadership teams simplify, clarify, and achieve their short-term and long-term goals.

In addition to starting and running three of his own companies in Turkey, Tom has worked with a diverse range of companies from start-ups to Fortune 50 companies. His 30+ years of global management and coaching experience help him quickly identify and then assist leaders in solving issues that keep a company from achieving optimal success—with the entire organization advancing as a cohesive team.

As a speaker, teacher, facilitator, and coach, Tom spends his time helping leadership teams implement EOS in their companies and delivering keynote addresses to audiences around the world. He is a Certified EOS Implementer®. He earned his BA from Hope College and MBA from the Fuqua School of Business at Duke University.

When not helping clients, presenting workshops, or delivering keynote addresses, Tom is most likely hiking in the mountains, traveling the world, or chopping wood at the lake.

Alex Freytag is the product of an entrepreneurial household. He has spent much of his business experience focused on his passion for being a hero to entrepreneurs. Between selling handmade James Dean t-shirts out of his locker in high school to becoming a Certified EOS Implementer, he has run or helped run five growth-oriented businesses before discovering the Entrepreneurial Operating System (EOS).

Drawn to EOS's simplicity and effectiveness, Alex has since devoted himself to helping others master this complete "way of operating" an entrepreneurial organization to help them get what they want from their businesses. An author and a sought-after speaker, Alex entertains, educates, and has introduced EOS to thousands of business leaders worldwide.

Alex resides in Columbus, Ohio with his wife, Christine, and their three children. He enjoys traveling, hiking, golf, scuba diving, and reading for pleasure.

ProfitWorks

Real. Simple. Results.

How do you harness your human capital, set priorities, and solve issues?

Imagine coaches Alex Freytag and Tom Bouwer helping you set your vision, gain traction, and create a healthy, functional team by implementing EOS.

EOS®
Entrepreneurial Operating System®

If you are frustrated by: a lack of control, poor revenue and profit, your people, little accountability, among other things...

...Tap into Alex and Tom's experience coaching

» 300+ companies
» More than 1200 transformational sessions
» Implementing EOS for 14 years

Keynotes.
Workshops.
Presentations.

Tired of speakers who just give nice theories?
Need real, simple, practical tools?

Tom Bouwer and Alex Freytag

use their extensive practical knowledge and
experience to engage your audience with the most
relevant content and easy-to-use tools.

What the Heck is EOS?

Your organization's success depends on EVERYONE pulling in the same direction. Understand EOS, become more engaged in the process, and take an active role to get what you want from your business.

Over 200,000 copies sold worldwide

Designed for all levels—owners, executives, managers, and employees.

Be sure to check out the sample chapter provided in this book.

Do you feel challenged when trying to engage employees to gain traction in your business?

"*Achieve Your Vision* is a crystal clear and profoundly useful book...a super-practical system for dropping the victim mentality and achieving real bottom-line results."

—Steve Chandler,
Best-selling Author, Motivational Speaker

Simple, proven tools implemented by thousands of companies along with real-life lessons learned from a life-long entrepreneur.

Available at

Made in the USA
Middletown, DE
14 November 2022

15002298R00094